Peter Gethers lives in New York City and Sag Harbor, New York, with his cat, Norton. He is a publisher, has written several television shows, films, newspaper and magazine articles, way too many memos, and is now hard at work on his third novel.

PUBLISHED NOV '92

EDITION R/P

PRINT N°. 41,000

COVER PTR ⌐ slw

The
CAT WHO
WENT TO
PARIS

PETER GETHERS

CORGI BOOKS

Corgi edition reprinted 1993

THE CAT WHO WENT TO PARIS
A CORGI BOOK   0 552 13837 1

Originally published in Great Britain by Doubleday,
a division of Transworld Publishers Ltd

PRINTING HISTORY
Doubleday edition published 1991
Corgi edition published 1992
Corgi edition reprinted 1992

This book is set in Bembo by
Falcon Typographic Art Ltd, Fife, Scotland

Corgi Books are published by Transworld Publishers Ltd.,
61–63 Uxbridge Road, Ealing, London W5 5SA, in
Australia by Transworld Publishers (Australia) Pty. Ltd.,
15–25 Helles Avenue, Moorebank, NSW 2170, and in New
Zealand by Transworld Publishers (NZ) Ltd., 3 William
Pickering Drive, Albany, Auckland.

Printed and bound in Great Britain by
Cox & Wyman Ltd., Reading, Berks.

To Dad. You're missed.

To Mom. You're appreciated.

To Janis. I can't believe you let me do this.

To Norton. What can I say? You'll be hand-fed
Pounce as long as I'm around.

Acknowledgements

First and foremost, thanks to Leona Nevler. All she did was come up with the idea for the book, think of the title, have confidence that I could write it, then come up with all the right suggestions to fix it. That's a good definition of a great editor.

Esther Newberg deserves a line or two (or a hundred) for convincing me this was a good idea and, just generally, being the perfect agent.

Kathleen Moloney went through the manuscript word by word, as a favour. That was invaluable.

I wouldn't have Norton if it weren't for my brother, Eric. There's no way I can even *try* to thank him for that.

Also thanks to everyone who let me write about them (whether they knew it or not).

Foreword

A few weeks ago, I made out my first-ever will. At thirty-six, it left me feeling slightly melancholy, more than slightly middle-aged, and somewhat sentimental. Looking to share my sentiment, I mentioned to my mother that I had – quite magnanimously, I thought – left my New York City apartment to my brother Eric's one-year-old son, Morgan. Instead of the expected motherly glow of affection and pride, she looked at me as if I were an insane person.

'Can you *do* that?!' she asked.

I didn't understand her wide-eyed confusion, especially since, on the scale of human accomplishment, my mother ranks her small grandchild somewhere between Mahatma Gandhi, Thomas Jefferson, and Bo Jackson.

'Why not?' I said, just a tad confused. 'I mean, I hope he doesn't get to use it for another forty or fifty years, but if he does, it'll go to Eric first and he can—'

'Did you say *Morgan*?' she interrupted.

'Yeah. Who else?'

'I thought you said *Norton*,' dear old Mom told me.

'My *cat*? You thought I left my apartment to my *cat*?'

'Well,' she said, in a particularly wise moment, and shrugged, 'with Norton, you never know.'

1

Before the Cat Who Went to Paris

This is a book about an extraordinary cat. However, the extraordinary thing about *any* cat is the effect it has on its owner. Owning a cat, especially from kittenhood, is a lot like having a child. You feed him, do your best to educate him, talk to him as if he understands you – and, in exchange, you want him to love you. He can drive you mad with his independence. He can, just as surely as a child, create a tremendous desire to protect him from anything bad. He is small, vulnerable, wonderful to hold – when he lets you. And he throws up on just about the same regular schedule.

Like children, cats exist on a separate and probably higher plane than we do, but like children, they must be at least partially defined by their relationship with their parents. And though they can do all sorts of amazing things such as hiding in the tiniest room imaginable and refusing to be found no matter *how* late you are for wherever it is you have to take them, they cannot write their autobiographies. That is left to humans. So this, as it must be, is also a book about people. And thus about relationships. And all sorts of other things cats have no business being involved with but can't seem to help themselves.

My involvement with a cat was strictly accidental. In fact, I had to be dragged into it kicking and screaming.

By way of example, a little over seven years ago, someone asked me to name ten things that I believed were truly self-revealing, deeply heartfelt and absolutely irrevocable. This person, a woman I was going out with, asked me to do this, I believe, because she thought I was a person without much emotion, without a lot of passion. She had, I also believe, been through way too many years of Upper East Side New York therapy in which she had made way too many lists like this. The fact of the matter was that I had plenty of emotion and plenty of passion. I just didn't have much for her. People often seem to fall into this trap in their relationships. They seem to feel that if someone doesn't do what he is expected to do, then there must be something *wrong* with him. This is a much easier way of getting through life, I suppose, than having to think there might be something wrong with the expectations or oneself or the world. Or life.

I did, finally and over my better instincts, make a list of ten things I believed were true about myself. This is another trap that people fall into in their relationships (which cats *never* fall into): we do a lot of stupid things just so we don't have to be alone.

Anyway, this is the list that appeared:

1. I will never vote Republican.
2. Love does not usually hold up to close inspection . . .
3. . . . except for baseball. I *love* baseball – watching it, listening to it on the radio, talking about it, reading box scores. I am a baseball junkie.
4. Life is basically a sad thing, with an even sadder ending, so anything that brightens up a moment along the way is OK. Especially if it's funny.
5. I don't like being a part of anything – a religion, a regular softball game, a corporation, a government, you name it. As soon as some*one* becomes some*thing*, I tend to think he or she is lost.
6. Friendship must be earned. It is too important to fritter away on someone who doesn't want it, won't reciprocate it or isn't worthy of it. As near as I can tell, people don't have all that much inherent value, but friends sure do.
7. There's very little cause for cruelty.
8. On the other hand, I'll pick entertaining and intelligent over nice any day of the week.

9. I don't care what anyone says: I think Meryl Streep's a lousy actress.
10. I hate cats.

In the years that have passed, a few of these irrevocable items have actually remained steadfast. Several have been altered somewhat, some bordering on the brink of unrecognizability. And there is one of the above that is so ludicrous it now seems inconceivable that it ever crossed my mind, much less made it through my mouth or found its way on to paper.

Numbers 1, 3, 6 and 7 remain absolutely unchanged.

Number 4 is basically sound, although I cannot be nearly so definite about the word 'anything'. There are terrifying things I did not conceive of when I made my initial list: oat bran, crack, *People* magazine cover stories on recovering alcoholic celebrities, wilding, sequels and Abe Rosenthal's 'On My Mind' column in *The New York Times*.

Numbers 8 and 9 are a little tricky. 8 now depends more and more on my mood and how hard my day was. And Meryl Streep's Australian accent really is astonishing.

Number 5 has changed somewhat. I have found something I am willing to join.

Number 2 clearly relates to Number 5, which will become much clearer as this book continues, and they both, amazingly enough, have changed because of Number 10.

Ah yes, Number 10 . . .

Well, now we've come to the youthful folly, a statement made in such ignorance it boggles the mind . . .

I, of course, have a cat now. Norton.

I treat this cat as very few animals – or people, for that matter – have ever been treated.

If he is asleep in the middle of the bed when it's time for my day to end, I sleep curled up in a corner of the mattress, happily braving stiff necks and bad backs so he remains undisturbed.

I take Norton everywhere I go. He's been skiing in Vermont, to a writers' conference in San Diego, to the best restaurant in Amsterdam, back and forth on a regular basis to Paris. At one of that city's premier hotels, The Tremoille, when my assistant calls to make a reservation for Mr Gethers, the desk clerk knows to ask: *'Avec son chat?'*

I bought a house in Sag Harbor, a real-life Bedford Falls of a town near the tip of Long Island, and though there were many other mitigating circumstances, the secret and overriding reason for the purchase was because my cat *loves* to run around in a yard.

I've had one girlfriend break up with me because she believed I liked Norton better than I liked her (which I did). And I once didn't go on a vacation with another girlfriend to my favourite resort hotel in America because they wouldn't accept small, very well-behaved felines.

I worry about him, I talk about him (and *to* him, I have to add) to the point of idiocy, and if he doesn't sleep within a crooked arm's reach of my pillow – which he doesn't about one day a week – then I don't sleep very well. I actually worry that I've done something to offend him.

I sometimes – and this is a particularly tough one to admit publicly – let him eat off my spoon. Usually ice cream or yoghurt. Chocolate's his favourite flavour, and it's a pretty funny thing to watch when he decides it's time to lick that sucker clean.

It is hardly a one-way street, however. He does all sorts of things for me that are fairly extraordinary for a cat.

He goes for walks with me. No leash. On a beach with no cars around to disturb him, he's gone up to two miles, walking anywhere and everywhere from ten feet behind me to three feet in front of me. His record in traffic is three blocks, which he does most Sunday mornings when I stroll to Sean's Murray Hill market in Sag Harbor.

Norton will wait for me anywhere, no matter where I leave him. If I'm at a hotel, I can dump him outside by the pool or in the garden, and let him play there all day or night long. When I go to get him, he will be nowhere in sight, but when I call or whistle for him, he'll meow exactly once, then leap out of his hiding place to rush to join me. I honestly believe I could drop him in the heart of an African jungle, leave him for a year, reappear, and as long as I could find the bush he was last seen scurrying under, he'd be there waiting for me.

He likes to roughhouse. His favourite game is to pounce on my hand when it's moving tauntingly under a sheet, wrestle it and try to eat it – but he will *never* bite or scratch any part of me that he recognizes as mine. If sometimes he gets carried away in the heat of battle and a claw accidentally isn't pulled in in time when my hand comes out from the linen, he will freeze at the sound of my yelp, put his paws over his eyes and bury his nose under the pillow in shame until I pat him on the head and assure him I'm OK.

He sits on the side of the tub when I take a bath.

If I, as I sometimes forgetfully do, close the door to a room, leaving Norton on the other side, he will howl and meow as if possessed until I open the door. He does not like to be left outside of anything I am inside.

He trusts me.

He is quite a comfort when I'm sad and makes being happy much more fun.

He has seen me through broken hearts and illness and death.

I love my cat, if you haven't got the drift yet.

He actually forced me to change my list of irrevocable self-realizations.

In doing so, he changed my life.

When a small grey animal does a little thing like that for you, how can you *not* let him sleep in the middle of the bed when he's tired?

2

The Cat Who Came to New York

Have you ever seen a Scottish Fold?

One cat book I read dared refer to the breed as a 'mutation'. What they are, in fact, are incredibly handsome cats whose ears fold over in half, forward and then down, giving them a vaguely owl-like look. Their heads tend to be rounder than regular cat heads and their bodies, at least all the ones I've seen, seem to be short, firm and trim. Officially they are a shorthaired cat, but I would unofficially place them somewhere in between a long- and a shorthair. They feel particularly soft and nice. Their temperaments range from sweet to sweeter. All of the ones I've met and spent time with are intelligent, though of course none have risen to the heights of brilliance that mine has.

They actually do come from Scotland. Apparently, the first one was discovered in 1961 at a farm near Dundee, by some people named William and Mary Ross. All of the fold-ear cats running around today can trace their pedigree back to Susie, which is what the Rosses named the first one they discovered.

The first time I ever heard of a Scottish Fold was when I got a phone call from my brother, Eric, who lives in Los Angeles. We talked about life (it seemed fine), work (since he's a screenwriter, it was hard, nasty and full of deceitful intrigue), women (they were getting younger) and our health (we were getting older). The conversation seemed to have run its course when he dropped the bombshell.

'Oh, yeah,' he said. 'Did I tell you I got a cat?'

If this were a screenplay, the words *Long Pause* would now appear in parentheses, because there was a long one. A real long one. In that long pause my eyes rolled back in my head, my mouth dropped open as far as it could stretch and I was certain the world had gone mad.

'You hate cats,' I reminded him when I was finally able to speak.

'I know,' was his response. 'But this one's different.'

I then heard the description of my first Scottish Fold, whom he'd named Henry. I have to say, I wasn't convinced.

'But you hate cats,' I repeated. 'We both hate

cats. We loathe and despise them. We always have and we always will.' By this time I think I was starting to whine. 'We like *dogs*.'

I could tell, even from three thousand miles away, that my brother was smiling that annoying superior smile he has when he thinks I'm saying something idiotic.

'You'll see,' he said again. 'This one's different.'

I have to sidetrack here.

At the time, my girlfriend's name was Cindy Wayburn. We'd been going together for three years or so, having quite a nice time. At one point, about six months earlier, Cindy had casually mentioned to me that she was thinking of getting a cat. I, just as casually, mentioned that if she did she might think about spending her nights in someone's apartment other than mine.

We argued, we discussed, we argued some more. She cajoled. I brought up my 'cats don't fetch' premise and we argued even more. She even took the tack that it would be good for *me* to have a pet. I'd made the mistake of mentioning to her once that I missed having an animal around the house, that it felt lonely without one.

'A pet, yes,' I said. 'A cat, no.'

'But you travel so much,' was her comeback. 'You couldn't have a dog. It would die in about two weeks.'

'I know,' I said. 'That's why I *don't* have a dog. But that still isn't convincing me that a cat is a good idea. A cat would die in about two weeks, too – because I'd kill it.'

'You've never even been around cats. You'd like them once you got to know one. And it would be good for you. You spend a lot of time at the beach house – you could have company. You wouldn't have to spend so much time talking to the old ladies who hang out at the grocery store.'

'How do *you* know I spend so much time talking to the old ladies? Who told you?' I thought this had been a well-kept secret. Every summer I spent a solid month writing at a beach house I rented in Fair Harbor, Fire Island. Cindy, during the years it was Cindy, would come out on weekends, and I'd toil alone during the week, insisting that I loved the solitude. But after three days of slaving away over the typewriter (this was before I dared to punch away at a laptop), I'd begin to miss human companionship. I'd start to make a few more phone calls than usual, beginning around ten-thirty in the morning. After six days, my friends would start to keep their phone machines on since most of them didn't have the time to spend helping me avoid doing my work. At the ten-day point, I'd finally break down and start making three trips a day to the Fair Harbor market. It was only two blocks from my house and there was usually a group of elderly housewives hanging out there, gossiping with the butcher and with each other. By my third season at the beach, I'd become a regular at the market. I knew everything there was to know about hundreds of people I'd never met. And best of all, I wasn't at the typewriter for half-hour stretches, three times a day.

'Have you ever lived with a kitten?' Cindy demanded, ignoring my pleas to reveal the Fire Island squealer.

'I've never lived with a snake, either. And I don't want to. I don't like them. Was it Frank, the butcher? Was he the one who told you?'

We went around in this adultlike manner for a reasonable amount of time – about seven hours – until eventually she decided that getting a cat for herself or for me wasn't going to be a plus in our relationship. To my great relief, our arguing ended and things went back on an even keel.

Until Cindy went to Los Angeles to visit her mother.

She wasn't particularly looking forward to the trip, since she didn't much care for her mother. Once a year, however, filial guilt won out over common sense and Cindy would go west and pay a visit. Mrs Wayburn – and I'll try to be as fair and objective as I can here – was an absolutely horrid woman who lived in some part of the outskirts of LA I'd never actually heard of, in a delightful little community called La Mobile Home Cité. If they'd had a slogan, it would have been 'Come Spend a Few Depressing Years With Us Before Your Internal Organs Start to Fail'. All in all, it was a great place to spend time if you didn't care about air, space, or ever looking at anything attractive.

This visit was worse than usual. After the second day, they had a huge fight. Cindy wanted to take her mother out to a fancy dinner, simply to be nice. Mom, in her typical upbeat way, said that all food tasted the same to her – like a lump of decaying, cold, grey clay – so there was no point in throwing money away on something as unpleasant as eating well. Cindy thought this was an unhealthy attitude, mentioned this to her mom, and the battle ensued. An hour after that, she was in my brother's house, crying and eating a delicious *tarte tartin* (my brother happens to be an excellent cook).

Eric was extremely nice to her, really cheered her up, and by the time she called me to say good night, she was in a terrific mood. Much better than could have been expected. So good, in fact, I should have been suspicious. She told me she was going to spend the next morning shopping with my brother, then would be on a mid-afternoon plane home. She'd decided she didn't want to see her mother any more, and with no mother responsibilities, she didn't want to stay in LA. The last thing she said before she hung up was, 'You won't believe how cute Eric's cat is. Wait till you see him.'

I hung up, deciding I could wait a pretty long time.

At eleven-ten the next night, my phone rang.

'I'm at the baggage claim,' Cindy announced. 'Are you awake?' Her voice had that special singsong quality it had when she was feeling particularly affectionate towards me.

'I'm awake,' I said, in much the same tone.

'I'll be there in thirty minutes.'

'I can't wait,' I told her. And, in truth, I couldn't.

Cindy had a key to my apartment and could bypass the various security buzzers and phones and TV cameras most people had to go through to get into my building. So thirty minutes later, I heard my front door open. When I came out of the bedroom, Cindy was standing by the door, grinning happily.

I went to kiss her.

'No,' she ordered. 'Stop.'

I stopped.

'I have something to show you.'

'You do?'

She nodded.

'Do I have to go to the hallway to see it?'

'No,' she said, still with the biggest grin I'd ever seen on her face. 'Stay there. Close your eyes. I'll tell you when.'

I stayed, I closed my eyes. I heard her 'when' and opened them.

Cindy was holding a tiny little ball of fur in her hand. One hand. It was so small, for a moment I thought she'd brought an extremely well-behaved mouse back from California.

But it wasn't a mouse.

It was a tiny, tiny grey kitten with a round head and funny-looking ears that folded forward and down. The kitten was sitting up in her palm, boldly swivelling his head around, gazing at all the sights in my loft apartment.

'You got yourself a cat?' I stammered weakly.

The kitten stopped swivelling his head, now

stared directly into my eyes and mewed. A quiet little mew right at me. And to this day I swear that he smiled.

'No,' Cindy said. 'He's not for me.'

'Who's he for?' I asked quietly.

When she didn't answer, I said, again quite softly, 'Cindy? Who's the cat for?'

When she burst out crying, I had a vague suspicion I knew the answer to my question.

I'd known for years that if I ever had a pet – I assumed a dog – I'd name him Norton. There wasn't even a close second choice.

My favourite name for an animal – and my favourite animal up to that point – was Yossarian, my brother's dog. Yossarian was, in my opinion, not just an incredibly cute cockapoo, which, for those of you who are strictly cat lovers, is half-cocker spaniel and half-poodle. He was also a genius.

He was never on a leash, not even in New York City. He would walk with you to the corner, stop, wait for you to cross the street, then trot along beside you. He would wait outside stores for you while you shopped. He was also extremely friendly and just generally had a kind of existential, world-weary air to him that made you believe he was capable of carrying on a very interesting drawing-room conversation. In French.

I got to take care of Yossarian once, for a stretch of about six months, when Eric was living in Spain. I was living in a fifth-floor walk-up in the West Village, a divey little apartment, and

Yossarian moved in with me. It didn't take long for me to realize that Yos wasn't wild about climbing up and down the five flights of stairs whenever he had to go for a walk. He especially wasn't wild about it in winter, when the snow and ice were already tough enough on his LA tenderized paws.

I'd had him perhaps all of a week when, to my horror, the little guy started limping. I noticed it as we were strolling down Greenwich Street. His right front paw was definitely curled up in front of him and he was favouring it. I went over to him, picked him up and checked him out. I couldn't find anything wrong, but he was looking at me in such a pathetic way, clearly the dog was in great pain. I set him down just long enough for him to do his thing, then scooped him back up, carried him back to my building and up the five flights to my apartment.

I decided not to panic. I figured I'd give it a few days, then if the limping continued, I'd take him to the vet.

Yos seemed fine in the apartment, perhaps moving around just a bit slower than usual. Once he'd get outside, though, the limping would start up. I'd have to carry him around, set him down when he had to relieve himself, then pick him back up and return to my apartment with the dog cradled in my arms.

On the third day of this routine – he was now limping slightly even in the apartment and I was caringly carrying him up and down the stairs three times a day – we went for our afternoon stroll. I set Yossie down on the snow, and since I was with a woman friend, she and I walked on ahead to give him some privacy. After about half a block, I turned back to see how my ward was doing. He was doing just fine. In fact, he was doing so well, he was racing around the sidewalk in front of my building, playing with another dog. I couldn't believe it. I mean, this dog was *moving*. Full weight on that right front paw.

'Yossarian!' I called.

The dog froze. Didn't move an inch. Then he looked down at the snow on the ground, looked at me, looked back down at his paw, which was resting on the snow, one more look at me, and his paw shot up in the air in a desperate attempt to replicate the pathetic position he kept it in when he was feigning his limp.

'Forget it,' I said. 'The free ride is over.'

If dogs can shrug, Yossarian shrugged, put his paw back down and resumed his frolic with his playmate. That was the end of the limp.

I wasn't the only one who felt that Yossarian was far more human than the normal quadruped, by the way. A few years ago, when he was thirteen years old and getting sickly, my brother had a 'roast' for him. About twenty people showed up with presents for the dog, Eric served food and drink and everyone proceeded to tell their favourite Yossarian stories. I called from New York just to make sure that someone told my 'limping' story, which was by then part of the Yossarian legend.

When, about a year after that, Yos died, I

promise you, everyone who was there that day was truly happy that they'd got to tell him how much he'd meant to them over the years.

Ever since Eric had taken the *Catch-22* name for this brilliant little dog, I'd been trying to come up with a comparable name for my future pet. Dunbar was a consideration, but it came from the same book, so I discarded it. McMurphy was a possibility, but then the movie version of *Cuckoo's Nest* came out and I hated it, so that was the end of McMurphy. I went further back in the annals of literature and quickly rejected everything from Falstaff to Tristram to Verloc, then moved on and rejected Malloy, Zorba and finally even Snoopy.

I considered Steed (or Emma, if it was a female) from 'The Avengers', but somehow those just didn't stay with me. Travis stuck around for about six months – that being the name of the character played by Malcolm McDowell in *If . . .* and *O Lucky Man!* – but then a friend of mine got a dog and named him Travis as in Travis McGee.

I switched to the sports field in a move of anti-intellectual desperation.

I couldn't name a pet Willie. What if some poor oaf thought I was naming it after Willie Davis or Willie Wilson or some other inferior imitation of the godlike Mays? I couldn't risk it. None of my other idols' names really lent themselves to being repeated over and over again while trying to coax a four-legged animal out from under the bed. Muhammad? Julius? Roger 'the Dodger' Staubach? No. Jim Brown? Forget it. I'd wind up with a pet who'd periodically throw me off a balcony. I was just about to settle for Clyde, figuring I would have a very cool pet who would never panic under pressure and would play great D, when, about two years before Cindy walked into my apartment with a cat, the name came to me.

I'm a television baby. I always watched it, I always liked it, when I grew up I even wrote for it. Sitcoms were always my fave (once 'Bronco Lane' and 'Sugarfoot' went off the air). From an aficionado's lofty view, there are only a handful of sitcoms that deserve the label 'great'. I'm not talking about campy 'Gilligan's Island'–type garbage. I'm talking great writing, great acting, great characters. 'Bilko' has to be near the top. Same with 'The Mary Tyler Moore Show' and 'The Dick Van Dyke Show' and, later, 'Barney Miller' and 'Taxi'. But there's one that's in a class by itself. The others aren't even close. Best characters, best fat jokes, best sets, best straight man (or woman, actually), best Grand High Exhalted Wizard and the two best performances in TV sitcom history. Obviously, I'm talking about 'The Honeymooners' and, like a flash, I had visions of one day – and then every day for years and years – being able to come home from a hard day's work, call out, 'Norton, pal o' mine, I'm home!' and see a little furry guy come leaping towards me, licking my face in a frenzy of joy.

As soon as this little cat mewed up at me from

Cindy's hand, I knew that Norton had finally arrived.

I knew one other thing, too. And this came in just as much of a flash as the name.

It was love at first sight.

It doesn't make sense. There's no explanation. It's never happened to me before or since with man, woman, or beast, and I don't know if it ever will again.

I started to get angry at Cindy. I wanted to yell. I began to sputter and to say things like, 'How could you do this!' I was all set to pace and wave my arms around in the air like a lunatic. But I wasn't able to do any of those things. I didn't have the opportunity. Cindy was busy doing her impersonation of Lucy when Ricky comes home after finding out she disguised herself as a painter to get an audition at the club. 'I thought you'd like him . . . *sniff* . . . Eric said you'd like him . . . *sniff* . . . I'm sorry . . . I thought . . . *sniff* . . . Unaughhhhwaaaaaaaaa . . .' I knew I wasn't going to get anywhere in that direction, so I turned to you-know-who. With my mouth still open, I looked into the little cat's eyes and I melted. Just dead away, gone, total mush.

Cindy, now switching to her Laura Petrie mode, trying not to cry but letting me know she might start again any moment, held out her hand and I took the kitten from her. Having absolutely no experience with babies of any species – human or four-legged – I held him kind of awkwardly. Cupping him in my right palm, which I supported with my left, I brought him closer to me, raising him up to my face until we were nose to nose. I don't think he could have been more than six inches long or weighed more than two pounds. He was a light, soft grey with irregular patches of dark grey circling his body. Bits of white spread across the top of his paws and ringed around his little black-and-orange nose. Three startling lines of black began right between his eyes and streaked all the way down his back, broadening by his tail so that his back half was darker than his front. His tail, even then, was very bushy, with black rings around it. It looked like a tail that could have belonged to a raccoon. His eyes were huge, twice too big for his head, oval and green. I had absolutely never in my life seen anything that was so cute, so independent, so smart or anything that had ever looked quite so much as if it belonged to me. He never flinched or shifted his gaze away from me. He simply mewed once more and licked me more or less on my right eyelid with a sandpaperlike tongue the size of a small bristle on a paintbrush.

'He's six weeks old,' Cindy said in a little bit of a hushed tone, drying her eyes. 'And there's something very special about him. I don't think he's just a normal cat.'

I switched him to my left hand and ran my right hand lightly over him, from his head to his tail, the first time I'd ever petted a feline.

'Of course he's not just a normal cat,' I said. 'How could he be? He's *mine*.'

The shopping Cindy had done with my brother, of course, was to go out and buy this little cat,

31

Norton. When she had seen what a Scottish Fold looked like, she flipped. She told Eric all about how she wanted to get a cat and how I wanted a pet but refused to consider a cat, and he, having known me for a much longer time than she had, told her they'd go looking the next morning.

They drove out to the Valley, to the breeder where Eric had got Lester. The breed was, at the time, relatively unknown but already on the expensive side. Eric had paid three hundred dollars for his. (Now, believe it or not, a good Scottish Fold will cost you up to fifteen hundred smackers.) He was a big believer in the theory that if you're going out to buy something, it's much better to spend as much money as possible and be as impractical as you can.

As luck would have it, the breeder had recently ushered in a new litter of Folds. She had too many Folds. Because they were so expensive, she didn't think she could sell them all before they got so big that they'd get underfoot. She knew Eric, she took a liking to Cindy, so she gave them one for seventy-five dollars, with the simple promise that they'd give the kitten the best possible home.

'Here, I'll give you my favourite,' she told them.

She picked a six-week-old cat out of a cardboard box and handed him over. Along with his breeding papers, she gave them an article that had appeared the week before in the *San Fernando Valley Register*. The story was on exotic breeds of cats and, as an example of the exotic Scottish Fold, there was a photograph of the cat Cindy was holding. For the use of the article, the kitten had been named Baby and the caption under his photo said, 'Unlike some deceptively named feline families – Himalayans, for example, have no tie to the mountains – Scottish Folds like this kitten, "Baby", actually originated in Scotland.'

'He's a star,' the breeder said.

'I sure hope so,' Cindy told her.

He certainly acted like a star on the trip home. Cindy was a bit nervous taking such a young animal on the aeroplane. She wasn't sure how he'd react, what he'd do to go to the bathroom, whether such a long flight would make him neurotic for the rest of his nine lives. She quickly found out he wasn't the neurotic type. She had him in a little box, but minutes into the flight, she lifted him onto her tray table just to check him out. He yawned, lay down and immediately went to sleep. She figured she'd leave him there until either the cat or the stewardesses started to freak out. Neither happened. The cat sat or slept on the tray, happy as could be, for the entire trip. The dread bathroom problem never came up. (As Norton has proved on many a flight since, he either has an abnormally strong bladder or an equally dominant sense of decorum. On this initial trip and on hundreds to come, he simply waited until proper facilities presented themselves.) Occasionally he would stretch, look around, then sit back down. He meowed only twice. Both times Cindy cooed at him and stroked him – and he made it very clear that that was exactly why he'd bothered to speak. The stewardesses fussed over him delightedly, brought him milk, even picked him up to show him off to various passengers. Through it all, the little kitten acted as if he'd logged as many miles as Chuck Yeager.

In the taxi from the airport to my apartment, he scrambled on the backseat over to the door handle, which he stood on, stretching up to peer out the window as the car drove him into Manhattan.

'It was weird,' Cindy said, as I held him in my hand. 'Not only did he have absolutely no fear, he acted like he knew where he was going – *and was looking forward to getting there.*'

The cat now wiggled a little bit in my palm, so I gingerly set him down on the floor.

'He'll be scared,' Cindy told me. 'Kittens are always scared of new surroundings. This place'll seem huge to him and that's frightening to a cat.'

Uh-huh.

My frightened kitten meandered over to a couch in my living room. Then he strolled over to the couch opposite it. Then he went back, halfway between the two, plopped down on the rag rug and went to sleep.

I watched his little chest moving up and down while he slept. I'd never seen anything conk out quite so quickly. I knew I had an imbecilic grin on my face, but I couldn't help it.

'Norton,' I called to him softly. 'Norton . . .'

The kitten's eyes opened slowly. First they were just a slit, then they held at half-open, then his head tilted and he was looking up at me.

I smiled at Cindy.

'Look,' I said. 'He already knows his name.'

3

The Cat Who Went to Fire Island

Most people think that owning a cat is a lot less of a responsibility than owning a dog.

They're wrong.

They're especially wrong if a particular owner happens to decide that a particular cat is so sensitive, intelligent and aware of what's happening that he has to be treated on a higher level than the owner's fellow human beings.

There actually is a certain logic to this. After all, people have *choices*. They do not have to be friends with someone they don't like or who mistreats them. They do not have to be alone if they choose not to be. (This is a general classification, remember: it does not necessarily apply to those people who don't use deodorant in the summer, think Sandra Bernhard is funny, or who idolize the Robert De Niro character in *Taxi Driver*.) They do not have to eat only when someone remembers to feed them. And, most of all, if the person they live with comes home late, most people do not have to worry that that person has been eaten by a predator.

Cindy thought I was going a little overboard with this last comparison, but *she* was the one who gave me a book called *The Natural Cat*.

She gave it to me because it was rather immediately apparent that Norton was not only breaking down my resistance to *him*, he was breaking down a lifetime resistance to his entire species.

First of all, it's very difficult to resist anything that is so vulnerable. And there are very few things more vulnerable than a six-week-old kitten. Second of all, he didn't *act* vulnerable, which is even harder to resist. He scrambled, he clawed, he nudged; he took over my apartment is what he did. Third of all, he took over *me*.

His first sneak attack in this regard came in the middle of the night.

Cindy and I had a very particular sleeping order. I always slept on the left side of my bed, she on the right. I slept on my side; she curled around my back with her arms wrapped around me.

We weren't sure whether Norton should sleep on the bed. We didn't know if he'd wriggle around all night, keeping us awake, a prospect which didn't much excite me. We also didn't know if he'd even *want* to sleep with us. Maybe we were too huge and frightening. So we decided to leave it up to him.

His first night, we heard him sliding around the living-room floor as we were falling off to sleep. It seemed as if he'd made his choice – he'd find his own bed. Fine with me. No problem. Everyone knew cats weren't as affectionate as dogs, anyway. He could sleep wherever he damn pleased.

I awoke in the morning, as usual a few minutes before Cindy. With my eyes half open, I listened for the sounds of a small cat at play. Nothing. A bit worried, I strained to listen more carefully. It seemed natural that a new-born kitten should be awake causing trouble. Still nothing.

Then I felt a very light stirring from my pillow and I rolled my eyes down to get a look.

What I saw was a small, grey ball of fluff, comfortably resting under my cheek and neck. He was awake, his eyes wide open, but he wasn't moving. Not an inch. He was staring straight at me, waiting for me to make my first move.

Without lifting my head, I slowly twisted my left arm, bringing it up so I could pet him. With two fingers, I stroked the top of his head, rubbing between his eyes down to his nose. He shifted, ever so slightly, stretching his neck so I could scratch under his chin. We stayed like that for several minutes, the cat stretched out luxuriously, the owner scratching away.

I felt pretty good.

He'd chosen me to sleep with. Not just the bed. Me. Not Cindy. *Me.*

It was *embarrassing* how good it felt.

I swivelled around to glance at Cindy. She was awake now, too, watching us and smiling.

Thus began a whole *new* sleeping arrangement. When Cindy spent the night, Norton would stay in the living room until we fell asleep. But every morning, when I awoke he'd be scrunched against my neck, partly under my cheek, absolutely wide awake, waiting for me to scratch under his chin.

If it was just the two of us – me and the cat, not me and Cindy – Norton would take Cindy's place before the lights went out. He'd lie in her spot on the bed, head on her pillow, body stretched out like a person, usually under the covers. I'd turn my back to him and he'd snuggle up there, exactly as Cindy did. In the morning he'd still be on her pillow, wide awake, staring straight at me, waiting for me to rise and shine. When I'd open my eyes, he'd move a few inches to me, lick my eyes or my forehead, then move to his under-the-cheek-and-neck position for five minutes of petting and scratching.

He never, ever, woke me up. Never, ever, meowed for breakfast. *A deux* or *ménage à trois*, he would stay quietly in bed until I was awake, wait until his morning petting, then he'd get up and join me for breakfast in the kitchen – one black coffee, one chicken and kidney in cream sauce de luxe.

His next sneaky little way of worming himself into my life was my own fault.

I wanted to show him off. (I knew that was a bad sign, but there you have it; there was nothing I could do about it.) So I started taking him places.

Not far away. Just to friends' apartments. He was, needless to point out, quite a hit, proving to be as fearless in these apartments as he was in mine, prowling and hopping around from room to room. Some of these friends had cats of their own and were a bit worried about possible confrontations. I couldn't imagine how anything – even a rival cat – could object to Norton and, as it turned out, I was right. Most of the time, the cat whose turf we were invading would immediately hiss and circle Norton, whom I'd have plopped down in the middle of the living room. Norton would peer over at the tough king of the castle, give him a look as if to say, 'Who are you kidding'; then he'd roll over on the ground and look as cute as an animal could look. The grown cat would, more or less, have no choice but to come over and be friendly. Otherwise he'd look like a warmongering idiot in front of his owner.

It seemed like too much of a bother, on these goodwill tours, to lug his carrier around the city, especially when he was so tiny, so I'd simply put on a windbreaker or a raincoat and stick Norton in the pocket. Walking a few blocks was no problem. He'd sit calmly, occasionally sticking his head out over the pocket's rim to peer around, then retreat back inside. He actually got pretty good at this form of transportation. Even on long subway rides to the Upper West Side. The noise didn't seem to frighten him; rather it intrigued him. The sudden jarring stops and starts struck him as something of a fun game. The only drawbacks were (1) the bums who, thinking they might be hallucinating, would want to touch him to make sure he wasn't the step before the pink elephants, and (2) the garrulous strangers who were positive that a cat in one's pocket was an open invitation to tell life stories, tales of woe or, worst of all, adorable pet anecdotes of their own.

On Saturdays, I started to get into the habit of taking him with me on my errands. He never squawked about this; in fact, I think he liked it. Most shops were happy to see his little head pop out and swivel around. In my local bakery he came away with quite a few scraps of cookies and sweet rolls and he developed a serious taste for jelly doughnuts; in the local grocery store he often lucked into pieces of cheese and the occasional chicken part. He'd even stay quiet – in an oversized pocket – for a relaxing brunch in a Village restaurant on a Sunday afternoon. A few waiters and waitresses wondered why I always ordered a glass of milk – a short, round glass if at all possible; if not, a tall glass and an empty saucer on the side – to go with my Mimosa or Bloody Mary, but no one ever said anything. To this day, I'm sure there are several *maître d*'s and busboys who talk about the bearded fellow who always left little puddles of milk under his seat. You'll just have to take my word for it that I was actually quite neat. Norton, however, is one of the sloppiest lappers I've ever seen. When thirsty, his tongue reminds me of nothing so much as one of those machines that swirls paint around, nearly at the speed of light, on small canvases so kindergarteners can create instant works of abstract art.

I got used to keeping my hand inside my coat on my travels about town, and constantly stroking this soft little cat. He got used to these hour- or two-hour-long adventures. When I'd leave the house without him – as I was forced to do far more often than I liked – he would look way too sad. As a result, it was taking me longer and longer to get out the door. (Have you ever spent five minutes explaining to a cat about your day's agenda and how it just wouldn't work if he came on your important meetings with you? Have you ever tried it when you have company? A word of advice: Don't.) Norton clearly didn't like being left behind. He much preferred being carried around in a pocket to spending the day dozing on the windowsill.

My only problem, other than my five- and ten-minute out-the-door soliloquies, was that summer was coming up. Even for Norton I didn't think I could wear an overcoat in the New York summer.

Meanwhile, since it was immediately apparent that Norton and I were joined at the hip (or the pocket, as the case may be), Cindy did two things. First, she got a cat of her own, a normal full-eared cat for whom she paid Bide-a-Wee five dollars. She named him Marlowe, as in Chandler and *The Big Sleep*, not the sixteenth century and *Tamburlaine*. I couldn't really object. I mean, here I was with my own cat who was sleeping on my head and for whom, twice in the first two weeks of our relationship, I'd stayed home from work so I could get to know him better. I no longer had a leg to stand on as far as cat-prevention was concerned. Besides, I liked Marlowe quite a bit. He was just as sweet as Norton. (In fact, in some ways, sweeter; it was clear from the beginning that Norton had a touch of the rebel in him. He liked to test me. Little things like scratching at the couch. To be perfectly honest, my attitude was that if scratching the couch gave him so much pleasure, let him scratch. It wasn't that big a deal to get a new couch every so often. But a horrified Cindy insisted that was no way to raise a kitten, so whenever Norton scratched, I would tell him 'no!' just the way Cindy told me I was supposed to. He was definitely smart enough to realize he was doing something wrong and would immediately respond to my warning. He would stop scratching at once and move about three feet away from the leg of the couch. Then, watching me all the way, he would, inch by inch, slink back to the leg, stick his paw out, and give the thing one or two good rakes. I would clap my hands, say 'no!' again, and he would scamper those three feet away. I'd turn my back and, two minutes later, hear the familiar scritching of claws on canvas. I must admit I was proud of this James Dean-like adventurous streak and secretly encouraged it, whereas Cindy loved the fact that *her* cat wouldn't *dream* of doing anything to upset her.) Marlowe was quite handsome in his own way, too, a beautiful dark coat streaked through with black and brown, though even Cindy had to admit he wasn't in my guy's league. He was also a much better jumper than Norton. Marlowe could do something that never

43

failed to amaze me. He could jump from the floor to the top of an open door and balance himself there. Norton used to eye this physical agility with some envy, I believe, though he soon realized his own limitations and comfortably settled for intellect over brawn. Overall, though, as truly nice as Marlowe was, he was *normal*. He was a cat. Norton was something more.

The second thing Cindy did was buy me the aforementioned book, *The Natural Cat*, so I could actually learn something about my animal. It's a wonderful little book and I quickly studied up on such things as how cats clean themselves and how they adjust to litter boxes and all the things cat owners around the world already know and don't need to read about here. To me, it was all fascinating, much like discovering a whole new culture. I had never heard anything purr before and I thought it was very possibly the most wonderful, soothing noise I'd ever listened to. I liked nothing better than having Norton stretch out on the bed or couch with me lying on top of him, the full weight of my head plunked down right in the middle of his body. He would purr and purr and purr in delight. I soon realized I was passing up reruns of 'The Rockford Files' in order to spend an hour listening to this motorboat sound.

I had also never seen fur on anything's back stand straight up or claws that retracted. I was particularly fascinated by his claws because, as much as he loved to scratch, his claws *never* came out when we were roughhousing. He made it quite clear that such a thing was unthinkable and I found myself touched and moved by his instinctive gentleness. In general, I was extremely interested in reading about the whys and wherefores and history of all such behaviour and physical reactions.

In the last chapter of *The Natural Cat*, the psychology of the feline is discussed. At some point in the chapter, it says to watch and notice: if you come home from work every day at six o'clock, when you arrive at the regular hour, your cat will be dozing contentedly in some comfortable spot. He will be relaxed and calm when he lifts his head up to welcome you home. HOWEVER: if you usually come home at six o'clock and then you don't come home until eleven or so, when you walk in the door your cat will be pacing up and down, nervously wondering if you've deserted and abandoned him. This is because his fifty million years of jungle instinct will have taken over and the cat is sure that you've been eaten by a predator. He has no idea you went for a drink with a co-worker, then hit a ballgame with a pal. The only thing he can conceive of is that you were minding your own business, lapping up some water from a lagoon, and some tusked animal weighing over two tons came along and bit you in half.

I started worrying about this. Not obsessively, not day in and day out. I wasn't that far gone. But if Cindy and I were out to dinner and it got past nine o'clock, I would start to get a little edgy.

'What's the matter?' she'd say.

'Nothing,' I'd respond. Then I'd glance at my watch nervously.

'What *is* it?' she'd want to know. 'You're wriggling. You only wriggle when there's something wrong.'

'It's nothing. Really. I'm just a little tired.'

'Do you want to go?'

'No, no,' I'd say. 'Absolutely not. I'm fine. Let's stay.'

Five minutes would pass and I'd nudge her under the table. 'Maybe we should go *now*,' I'd whisper. And we would, much to Cindy's confusion and annoyance.

When we got to my place, Norton would be standing by the front door, looking, I was sure, incredibly stressed out. I'd pick him up, pet him for a while, reassure him that his dad had survived another day in the nasty jungle, tell him what a great dinner he was in store for, then sigh with relief and exhaustion that a crisis had been averted.

After a couple of weeks of this, Cindy figured out what was going on. She took *The Natural Cat* off my bookshelf and threw it away. She also forbid me to read anything or learn anything more about cats. She decided it was too dangerous.

The germ had already been forming, but this whole predator business put it over the top. I was beginning to think that, whenever and wherever possible, I should just take Norton with me. I would be a lot more relaxed and I was pretty sure he'd enjoy tagging along with his dad rather than sitting around my apartment all day. The short pocket trips worked OK. Why not the more major excursions?

Cindy wasn't as supportive as I'd hoped. She told me I was crazy.

'You can't just take your cat on trips all over the place,' she informed me.

I didn't understand why not. 'He likes me. He's pretty calm. He goes to your house OK. What's the big deal?'

'The big deal is he's a *cat*. Cats don't like things like that.'

'*He* does.'

'He's a kitten. He'll go along with anything. When he gets bigger, he's going to hate it.'

'I don't think so,' I said. 'I think he'll go for it.'

'It just doesn't work that way,' she said, shaking her head.

'Well, I'm gonna try it,' I told her. 'I like him. I like being with him. I don't see why he won't like being with me.'

In fact, I had a place in mind I knew he would love to visit.

Fire Island is about an hour's drive or train ride from Manhattan. As mentioned, I rented a house there every summer, in the town of Fair Harbor. It was a wonderful little guest house, painted a deep sky blue; one room, comfortably furnished, with a Pullman kitchen and a sleeping loft. It had a cosy deck, which, even though the beach was only fifty feet away, I could rarely bring myself to leave. The entire island is approximately twenty-six miles long

47

and about two blocks wide from bay to beach. There are many different little communities, each with distinctly separate rules and equally separate lifestyles. The rules range from *No Eating in Public* in one particularly crowded community to *No Campfires on the Beach* in a particularly cautious community to *No Rich People's Seaplanes Landing Here or We'll Blow Your Head Off* in one particularly blue-collar community. The lifestyles range from '*Wild-Divorced-Heterosexual-Manhattanites-Discoing-the-Night-Away-in-Desperate-Search-of-a-New-Year's-Eve-Date* to *Boring-Please-Don't-Give-My-House-a-Funny-Name-I'm-Here-to-Relax-Not-Talk-to-Strangers* to *If-You're-Not-Gay-and-Haven't-Rented-Can't-Stop-the-Music-at-Least-Three-times-Don't-Even-Bother-to-Step-Off-the-Boat*. I was in one of the Boring–Please–etc.–etc. communities and I liked it fine. In fact, I thought it was pretty close to heaven. There was one restaurant, which I dined in once a summer, a little grocery store, which, as mentioned, I went to a little too often, and a five-and-dime run by a woman who used to be a Rockette. (She was kicking when *The Men*, Brando's first film, played there.) There were a lot of nice families around me with a lot of nice kids. Best of all, cars aren't allowed on Fire Island. If you don't want to walk, you take a bike. If you don't want to do either of those, your only other choice is to sit in the sun and listen to the waves lap up to the shore. It seems like a place, with its wooden boardwalks and water taxis and everybody-knows-everybody-else feel, that time has forgotten. Above all, it is safe. Fire Island makes you feel that nothing bad can happen there, certainly nothing worse than, if you're a kid, falling down and skinning your knee, or if you're an adult, having too much to drink at a cocktail party and winding up in bed with a fat woman named Naomi. Which is why I thought it was the perfect place for Norton to make his first excursion.

Once Cindy understood I was quite serious and that there was no way I was leaving my cat home alone for a whole weekend, she decided to give it a try with Marlowe. She didn't want him to grow up feeling like the neglected stepchild.

For our first trip *en famille*, we took Tommy's Taxi, a van service that picks you (and a lot of other yuppified weekenders anxious – and loud about it – to leave the city) up in Manhattan and drops you off at the Fire Island ferry. We bought a regular pet carrying case, a plastic one with metal bars on the top. Since both cats were so little, we figured one case would be plenty big enough.

We met the van at Fifty-third and First Avenue, loaded our bags on, then climbed aboard and made ourselves as comfortable as we could amidst the jewellery and designer clothes and exposed body parts. The cat case sat on my lap.

About fifteen minutes into the trip, I decided that it couldn't possibly be very comfortable curled up inside a portable pet prison, so I opened it an inch and stuck my hand in to reassuringly pet both guys. Marlowe didn't respond. His nose was buried in a corner and he was trying his best to pretend he had been in a coma for

49

about three weeks. Norton, however, scurried over to my fingers and began shoving his nose up against them. I stroked him for a minute, then when Cindy was looking away, staring rather horrifiedly at a pair of dangling gold earrings that spelled out a phone number – three numbers hanging from the left ear, four hanging from the right; I assume the woman wearing them had the area code tattooed some place I didn't want to know about – I lifted Norton out of the box and quickly shut it back up.

He looked up at me gratefully and meowed. At the sound, Cindy glanced over. When she saw the kitten on my lap, she rolled her eyes.

'I know, I know,' I told her and tried to pretend that I sympathized with her hard–hearted approach to pet travel. 'But he looked so unhappy in there.'

'He wasn't unhappy,' she told me. 'He's a cat. *You* were unhappy because you weren't holding him.'

I glanced down at Norton, who was curled up in a ball on my lap, his head resting on the back of my hand. I nodded at Cindy, acknowledging that her assessment was correct.

'At least move your hand,' she told me. 'You can't be comfortable sitting like that.'

'I'm all right,' I told her.

'You're comfortable?'

'Well . . . not exactly. But . . .'

'But what?'

'But *he* looks so comfortable.'

'I think,' Cindy said, 'I may have made a mistake.'

★

50

The rest of the trip went according to form. Marlowe cowered in the box, doing his best Helen Keller impersonation; Norton wound up inching his way up my arm and perching on my shoulder, watching the countryside slide by as we sped along the LIE.

One of the things I liked best about his position on my shoulder was that it didn't ever seem to occur to him that he couldn't just push me out of the way or take up whatever space he wanted to take up. That's where he wanted to be so that's where he belonged. And I had to agree. It only seemed fair. He was little; he was being lugged around not by his own choosing; he had no idea where he was going or why. If he wanted to sit somewhere and at least get a good view, how could I complain? I felt – and I think this is one of those clever things that cats somehow manage to do – *honoured* by the fact that he chose me to be his piece of comfortable furniture.

In fact, not only wasn't I complaining, I was mesmerized watching Norton on his first trip in the van. He spent almost the entire hour staring out the window, hunched forward, his neck craning, his nose pressed against the glass. Something fascinated him out there, though I sure couldn't tell what. Every so often he'd turn to look at me and his eyes were full of questions. He'd stare at me until I felt ridiculously ignorant, and I'd whisper, 'What? What do you want to know? *What?* Tell me!' When it became plain that I couldn't help him, he'd turn back to the window and continue his vigilant watch.

The thing is, it's not as if he were watching a flickering fire in a fireplace, unfocused and glazed by simple noise and movement. For Norton, this was hardly a vacuous way to pass the time. He wasn't *just* staring. His eyes were alert, constantly moving, his head shifting back and forth as if he were keeping track of a baseline to baseline rally at an exciting tennis game.

He was so *interested*. And it made me incredibly curious. I acted like a proud father whose son was about to win a sixth-grade spelling bee. I kept nudging Cindy, not saying anything, just flicking my eyes toward Norton as if to say, 'Will you look at him? Is he smart or what?'

Several people on the van actually stopped talking about themselves long enough to notice that there was a kitten perched on my shoulder, a kitten with folded ears who seemed to be unduly interested in the landscape of Long Island.

A couple of them reached over to pet him. Norton took the attention with what I would come to know as his typical *laissez-faire* reaction to adoring crowds. He didn't shrink away or scurry back into his carrier. Nor did he rub his nose affectionately against unknown palms or offer encouragement in any way. He simply sat there and took the cooing and petting and compliments as stoically as he could. At some point he turned to me, since we were basically at eye level to each other, and the expression on his face said, 'It's all right. This is just the price I have to pay for being me.'

I nodded at him knowingly, and when the petting stopped, he snuggled a few inches closer, turned away from the strangers, buried his face against my neck, closed his eyes and went to sleep.

Marlowe, who in the van had certainly been, if not happy, quiescent, did not take well to the twenty-minute ferry ride from mainland Bay Shore to Fair Harbor on the island. He wouldn't move an inch in the carrier and when Cindy went to pet him reassuringly, he drew away from her touch. I think, if he hadn't been as truly sweet as he was, he might have hissed at her. But things hadn't quite reached that tragic level.

Norton, of course, only made matters worse because he took to the open sea (or, at least, the open bay) as if he were related in some way to the Popeye family.

As in the van, his nose went right to (and through) the metal bars at the top of his carrier and he made it plain as day he wanted out. So, once again, I reached in, scooped him up and set him on my lap.

Within a few experimental minutes, we found the position we both liked best: me with my left leg crossed over my right knee at a ninety-degree angle, Norton with his body on my right thigh and his head resting on my left foot. (For him, that's still his favourite travelling position, although as he's got older and bigger, his body and head now go from right thigh to left knee. For me, as *I've* got older and my joints creakier and creakier, it's less and less comfortable. Of course, I'm too well trained to change. I much prefer creaky joints to a disgruntled travelling companion.)

He also, about ten minutes into the crossing, decided the water was practically as interesting as the highway. With me holding the middle of his body as firmly as I could, he perched himself back on my shoulder, with his front paws resting on the ferry's railing.

Cindy was a little nervous seeing him in such a precarious position and I must admit so was I. Believe me, I had visions of myself diving overboard in search of a floundering kitten. But I did have hold of him. And even more of a but, I simply had a very strong sense that this particular cat would not do anything as rashly crazy as jump off my shoulder into the freezing bay. I don't know why I had such faith in him, except to say that he more than justified it. I expected him to behave in a certain way right from the beginning and he almost always did. I've left Norton in cars with the doors open, in airport waiting rooms while I went off to confirm tickets, in restaurant chairs while I went to use their toilets. Not once do I ever remember him running or jumping or hiding.

We got some awfully strange looks on that boat: a boy and his seafaring kitten. Then in twenty minutes we were back in land. We'd been in a taxi, a van and a ferry. We'd braved rush-hour traffic, the spray of sea salt and crazed sun-worshippers. The premier leg of Norton's first real journey was complete.

4

The Cat Who Commuted

Norton took to outdoor life immediately. It was a little frightening how easy it was to begin thinking of him as a country squire.

We took both cats into the little beach house and flipped open the carrier. Marlowe – poor guy; I hope no one ever reads this to him because he's going to get one hell of a serious inferiority complex – wouldn't come out. If I hadn't spent many more months in his company and *seen* him out and around, I'd venture to say he might *still* be in that box. Norton, on the other hand, had his new pad all checked out in a matter of minutes. He was the second coming of Tony Bill in *Come Blow Your Horn*.

He sniffed the miniature house out thoroughly – around the couch, over to the Pullman kitchen, up the ladder stairs to the sleeping loft. After exploring the upstairs, he stuck his head over the edge of the loft to look down at us and I knew exactly what he had in mind. When we made eye contact I shook my head only once, but firmly – and I'm convinced that's why he took the stairs back down to the living-room floor, one little jump at a time instead of one great twelve-foot leap. I knew (and he knew) he could have done it. But I knew (and I'm sure he knew it, too) I probably would have had a heart attack.

Back downstairs, he checked out the bathroom, hopped onto the rim of the tub, slid down inside it. It was vinyl and very smooth, far too slippery for a kitten his size to easily leap back out, so when he began meowing impatiently I had to go fetch him. This became a fairly regular ritual until he grew to a more adult size and could get out of his own scrapes. At least once a day I'd hear a plaintive meowing echoing from the bathroom and have to go to the rescue. I must admit, partly to pay him back for dragging me away from work or fun or bed, partly because it was extremely funny to watch, I'd usually give him three or four tries on his own. He'd see me, try to scamper up the wall of the tub, not make it, and slide back down towards the drain. After a few unsuccessful attempts, he'd meow sharply, just once, to let me know the game was over and he wanted my help – *now*. He was not humiliating himself for my enjoyment any longer.

Norton particularly liked the walls of the beach house, which were covered with a burlap cloth. Quite attractive, no doubt, but also very handy for climbing.

While Cindy and I were doing our best to coax Marlowe out of the carrier, we heard a very quick ripping noise – actually five or six quick ripping noises – and turned around to find Norton up near the ceiling, his claws clinging to the wall fabric.

I, of course, thought this was the greatest thing I'd ever seen. I was ready to rank Norton with Columbus, Tom Sawyer, John Glenn and the first guy who ever ordered mail-order meat on my list of great adventurers. Cindy, luckily for my bank account, quickly pointed out how expensive it would be to completely refurbish every wall in the house. So we quickly pulled Norton down and tried to discourage this particular excitement, although it, too, became something of a regular occurrence.

We next went out of our way to orient our adventurous cat. A litter box was set up in the bathroom and we carried him to it so he'd be unable to use ignorance as an excuse for any accidents. (It turned out that in three years on Fire Island, he never *once* used a litter box. Outside, one giant sandbox was at his disposal, and I think he took great satisfaction in relieving himself in the freeing manner of his ancestors.) We also put food and water down for him and Marlowe – separate bowls, of course – but we figured Marlowe was *weeks* away from eating. Norton acknowledged the food with a quick bite or two of kibble, but his mind was elsewhere. He wanted the great outdoors.

Although he went straight for the screen door, he was still such a small kitten – not yet three months old – Cindy thought that, for health reasons, we shouldn't really let him loose outside. He was too young to be exposed to all those unknown germs and ticks and other strange things that abound in nature and that I couldn't even bring myself to think about. But he seemed so anxious to take off for parts unknown . . .

I had a solution. It was a perfect summer day, so we quickly changed into our formal Fire Island wear – shorts, no shoes, no shirt for me, tank top for Cindy – made ourselves some iced tea and began Step One of turning Norton into an outdoor cat. We put a blue collar on him – quite distinguished-looking nestled in his grey fur – and got a long, long string, maybe thirty-feet long, from the Rockette lady. We used the string to make an impromptu leash, carried Norton onto the porch and tied him to the handle of the door.

Minus Marlowe, who still hadn't budged from his portable prison, Cindy and I took our iced teas – by the way, these were nonalcoholic iced teas; this is worth explaining because we'd learned that, for some unknown reason, in bars and restaurants anywhere on Long Island, if you just order iced tea, they give you something with enough alcohol in it to topple an elephant – sprawled into our madras beach chairs, and waited to see what would happen.

We didn't have to wait long.

Norton needed a few seconds to get his bearing. This was a little different from being transplanted into a strange living room. This was like being picked up by Brian Dennehy in *Cocoon* and going for a stroll on a strange planet.

First he went into a crouch. He glanced around nervously, as if waiting for something to pounce on him. Then he relaxed a bit. He took a step forward, still staying fairly alert to the potential for danger. His nose twitched, taking in the hundreds of brand-new odours, and his folded ears switched from side to side, hearing all sorts of things, like birds and crickets and bees, that he had no idea ever existed. Then a great thing happened.

Norton suddenly sprang into the air in a joyous leap. Baryshnikov would have been jealous of his form. He landed on his padded feet and went right back up, this time swatting at the string, which lay stretched out before him. A meow came out of him, but not a normal meow. This one sounded suspiciously like 'whooooppeeeee!'

It took maybe thirty seconds for my cat to race exhilaratedly all around the deck. It took me maybe thirty *minutes* to unwind the string – which was now tangled up under a chair, around a square outdoor table, around another chair, twice around Cindy's ankles, over and then back under a third chair, somehow wrapping around the table again before coming to a sudden stop somewhere in the middle of the deck as the leash ran out of slack.

Norton couldn't move an inch. By the time I'd managed to straighten things out, he was raring to go again. And go he did. Another thirty seconds later, I was doing my best to unwrap him from his string straightjacket. Cindy couldn't stop laughing, Norton couldn't stop running and I couldn't stop unwinding. All three of us were as close to happy as it's possible to get.

Within a couple of weeks, we had the routine down cold.

Thursday evenings, pack one bag each, load each kitten into his own carrier – we'd splurged for comfort's sake; *their* comfort – catch the five-thirty Tommy's Taxi and the 7 p.m. ferry to Fair Harbor. Marlowe would hunker down in his carrier, emerging only when he was safely inside our house. Norton would spend the van ride on my shoulder, staring out the window, and the ferry ride on my lap, leaning up against the railing. Once we hit land, he was beginning to squirm and think seriously about jumping out of his carrier. I knew it wouldn't be long before he'd be prowling the island on his own.

I'd bought a new travel case, perfect for him, easy for me. It was really meant for dogs, but he was quite comfortable in it and seemed to like it better than the old one. It was a soft cloth shoulder bag with a hard strip underneath it for support. There was a mesh patch in front so the animal could breathe and see out. Norton didn't need the mesh to see or breathe, because I never zipped the thing closed. I just stuck him in and hung the bag on my left shoulder while he sat there, head swivelling in every direction, taking in every single sight, sound and smell. It wasn't long before I didn't even have to pick him up and put him inside. When it was time for us to take a trip, I'd simply lay the bag on the floor and he'd step right in and settle himself there.

After a month of weekends spent mostly trying to untie string from every available item on our deck, we decided it was time to turn the cat loose. My landlord, whose family shared the front deck with us, was complaining. Their bicycles were so tightly wrapped in string by this point, they looked as if they were bike mummies excavated from Tut's Tomb.

On the chosen weekend, Cindy and Marlowe had to stay in the city. One of Cindy's best friends was in from out of town, and they decided to have an official GNO (Girls' Night Out). The whole wild works – non-diet Cokes, oil on their salads, loud public discussions of bladder infections. Norton and I were on our own, bacheloring it up.

Friday night, in Tommy's Taxi, I happened upon a startling and, in years to come, useful revelation. It had always struck me as quite odd that none of the revelling weekenders in the van or on the ferry ever paid much attention to the fact that there was an incredibly cute cat on my shoulder, doing incredibly cute things. I didn't expect banners or original songs about 'A Cat Named Norton':

> Who's the cat with the floppy ears?
> Who's the cat who ain't got no fears?
> Who's the cat doin' all the cavortin'?
> That ain't no cat – that's Norton!

– or anything like that, but I did expect the occasional 'What a cute cat!' or 'Is he always this good?' or 'What happened to his ears?' No. Usually I got nothing.

Well, this Friday I was riding along as usual, immersed in the *Post* sports section, cat on my shoulder studying the LIE landmarks, when a woman behind me, wearing a sweatshirt that read 'Life's a Beach', said, 'What kind of cat is that?'

'A Scottish Fold,' I explained. 'His ears fold in half. See?'

'He's amazing.'

Smiling, I went back to the sports section.

'Excuse me,' the woman sitting next to me said. She had on a T-shirt that said, 'Life's a Beach'. 'What kind of cat did you say he was?'

'Scottish Fold,' I repeated. 'See? His ears fold like this.'

'He's beautiful.'

'Thank you.'

'Is he always this well behaved?'

'Always,' I said proudly.

Back to the sports pages.

'Is that a Scottish Fold?' the woman in front of me asked, turning around to smile at me. She *didn't* have on a T-shirt that read 'Life's a Beach'. But the guy sitting next to her did.

'Uh-huh,' I nodded.

''Cause his ears fold like this.'

'Uh-huh.'

'He's so *cute*.'

'I know.'

'Is he always this good?'

As a person who's always prided himself on being an acutely sharp observer of human behaviour, naturally enough I had absolutely *no* idea why, all of a sudden, Norton's ears were the main topic of the car ride. I had zero concept of what was different from past rides.

It wasn't until I was on the ferry that it hit me.

We were on the upper deck. Norton was peering fixedly at the gulls swooping around the waves. I was munching on a take-out order of fried clams, a specialty of Porky's, the wonderfully divey pub by the ferry.

I was single this trip.

That was the difference.

No one wanted to bother admiring my cat when I was sitting next to an attractive woman I was obviously attached to. But this night there was no Cindy. So all of a sudden, Norton was the perfect conversation starter.

I was mildly stunned. I'd never really seen myself as the object of a vanful of women's lust and desires. And I'd certainly never viewed Norton as bait to be trolled. Were times so bad that people wouldn't even *talk* to someone unless they wanted something? Like a mate for life? It was amazing. It was . . . .

As if on cue, a hand swooped down in front of me and plucked a clam – *my* clam – from the styrofoam plate.

I looked up to see a reasonably attractive woman, late twenties, holding the clam in her fingers. She was wearing – remember, this goes back a few years now – a *Flashdance*-type T-shirt. Over the course of the summer, I was going to become far too familiar with this look. (One of the amazing things about a sleepy little place like Fire Island being so close to Manhattan is the way fads sweep in and take over the entire island. My own personal favourite fad is a game called Kadima. It might also be called The Stupidest Game Ever Invented. It consists of one wooden paddle per player – of which there are usually two or three – and a hard black rubber ball. The object of the game is to stand ape-like on the beach, preferably in the middle of a particularly crowded section, where you can annoy people who are trying to mind their own business and have a good time. One player hits the ball to another person, not letting it touch the sand. There's no net, no out of bounds, no points, no rules other than what I've reported. What there *is* is a really loud, annoying noise that echoes every time ball hits paddle. Sounds like a lot of fun, doesn't it? Believe me, that summer Kadima was good for *hours* of entertainment on the ocean's edge.)

Anyway, back to the clam thief.

Her T-shirt was intentionally torn at the neck, revealing a darkly tanned shoulder (with a lot of flesh to tan) that had a tiny tattoo on it. I had an irrational fear that if I got too close to the tattoo, it would say, in micro letters, 'Life's a Beach'. So I averted my eyes, or at least refocused them on the clam.

'I knew that anyone with such a cute cat,' she began, 'wouldn't mind sharing his food. I'm *starving*.'

She showed me all her teeth in the friendliest smile I'd ever been on the receiving end of. It would have been more effective if her gums hadn't gone from her forehead nearly to her knees.

'May I have my clam back, please?' I asked her politely.

Her teeth sparkled again, only this time she popped the little fried sucker right in between the uppers and lowers.

'What kind of cat is that?'

I didn't answer. I was too busy watching her chew.

'How come his ears are down? Is he afraid?'

I shook my head. She swallowed. I watched the little bulge in her throat slide down out of view.

'Did you sedate him? How can he just sit there like that?'

Then she moved. Her bejewelled, tan fingers reached towards my plate again. This time my hand went up to meet hers. To her surprise, our fingers locked for a moment. But she managed that dazzling smile again. The smile faded somewhat when I said the words 'Touch another clam and die.'

I'm pretty sure she thought I was kidding, because she tried to disentangle her hand and make another go at my dinner.

'I don't want to be rude,' I said, in my best quiet Clint Eastwood impersonation, 'but I'm extremely hungry. I bought these clams so I could eat every single one of them, except for the ones I give to my cat. I don't mind if he reaches down and takes one because I know him. But I don't know *you*. So if you try to get to them, I'm afraid I'm going to have to find out where you live, sneak over in the middle of the night and break your thumbs.'

I did everything but say, 'Are you feeling lucky, punk?' It seemed to do the trick.

She backed away slowly – clearly she'd been flirting with the Ted Bundy of the ferry set – and disappeared into the crowd.

I looked down at the cat draped over my shoulder. He looked back at me and meowed.

'I know what you mean, pal,' I told him. 'I don't think we're ready for the singles' scene.'

The next morning was D-Day. Norton was about to hit the shore.

He knew it, too. Don't ask me *how* he knew, but he did. I've come to expect this from him. He always seems to know when a big event is upon us: if I'm going on a trip, if *he's* going on a trip, if something particularly sad has happened, if something particularly festive is about to happen. If I didn't know better, I'd swear he keeps a calendar hidden somewhere in the apartment. Because as he got more and more used to going away to the beach for the weekends, his morning routine even changed. Mondays through Thursdays, we'd go through our wake-up cuddling and then, as I dragged myself out of bed, Norton would race to the kitchen, jump up on the counter and wait impatiently for me to feed him. On Fridays, he'd race along the same path – off the bed, through the bedroom door, around the corner, sharp right, cut through the living room, past the front door, into the kitchen – only he'd skid to a sudden stop at the front door and wait there eagerly. On Fridays he didn't even care about breakfast. He just wanted to hit the open road.

On the day of his first outdoor solo expedition, the moment my eyes popped open in the morning, my guy was out of bed, waiting at the front door of the Fire Island house, glancing back repeatedly to see what was keeping me.

Still rubbing sleep out of my eyes, I pulled on a pair of shorts, climbed down the stairs of the loft and met him at the door. I hesitated. For one brief melancholy moment I had a vision of Norton on the side of an endless road, thumb out, heading far away in search of fame and glory. I composed myself, remembered that he didn't *have* a thumb, then I swung the screen open. Norton *didn't* hesitate. He scooted outside. In the blink of an eye, he was gone, racing across the yard, racing right back, disappearing in a flash under the deck.

I realized I had two choices. I could act like a total lunatic and tail him outside, try to follow him around wherever he went and keep an eye on him. Or I could be a rational, sane man: relax, make myself a pot of strong French Roast coffee with just a dash of cinnamon, get the newspapers, read about the fascinating events of the day, then go for a healthy, invigorating morning swim. It seemed like an obvious choice.

I decided to follow Norton.

He was having the absolute time of his life. Frolicking, chasing birds and squirrels – not catching, just chasing crawling through the grass on his belly, chomping on flowers and generally enjoying his new role of jungle beast on the prowl.

After half an hour or so, I decided he was safe and sound, more than able to cope on his own with the great outdoors, so I went back inside to attend to some people-related chores such as trying to write a book and earn enough money to pay for Norton's summer house.

I never *really* worried. I knew he'd stay fairly close to home or, at least, wouldn't go so far away that he couldn't find his way back. Periodically, I'd step to the front door or back window and call his name, just checking up. I'd hear one crisp meow in response, letting me know all was well, then I'd go back to work.

At lunchtime I decided to head to the market (I'd forgiven them for ratting on me to Cindy). Going for the surprisingly mature route, I didn't even check up on Norton. I figured he wouldn't miss me for the twenty minutes I'd be gone, so why bother him? I didn't want him to think I was an overprotective dad. Feeling as proud as a father whose son has just got his driver's licence and is driving away on his first date, I made a list of what I needed to buy and took off.

I was three-quarters of a block towards the market when I first heard it. A faint growling of a meow, a little whiney in fact. I took another two steps, heard it again. *Brrrrrrmeowwwww*.

I stopped, turned my head. Norton was in the middle of the sidewalk, twenty feet behind me. He was trying to follow, but I was walking too fast.

'What are you doing?' I asked. 'Go back to the house.'

Again I headed for the store, managing to take all of two steps before hearing a much more insistent meow. When I turned, Norton had scampered a few feet closer.

'Then come on,' I called. 'Let's go.'

And much to my astonishment, he ran up until he was about five feet behind me. Then he stopped. 'Come on,' I told him. 'I'll walk slow.' But he wouldn't budge any farther.

I took a few more steps, glanced behind me. He was following – but he stopped when I stopped. I went a few more steps, glanced. He'd kept pace.

I walked the rest of the three blocks to the market and Norton followed, always staying five feet behind, every few feet meowing to let me know he was still there. Several Fair Harborites passed by and stopped to stare in amazement. I acted as if there were nothing at all unusual about the world's cutest kitten going for a lunchtime promenade with his favourite person.

Twice, people on bikes zoomed past and Norton froze. But he never panicked. Once they were gone, I just had to reassure him that everything was OK, that bikes were only an occasional hazard here in the real world; then he'd resume his faithful trot, taking my word that I was watching out for his best interests.

In a few minutes we were at the entrance to

the market, where there were about ten times the number of people Norton had ever seen in his entire life. Kids were racing around playing tag, bikes and skateboards were skidding to and fro, several people with 'Life's a Beach' T-shirts were trying to impress several other people with *Flashdance* T-shirts. Even for Norton it was a bit much.

As we approached, I wasn't sure what to do with him. See if he'd stroll inside and peruse the aisles with me? Pick him up and carry him? Ask someone to keep an eye on him while I shopped – a ten-minute cat sitter?

Norton ended my pondering and took matters into his own paws. After sizing up the situation, he darted past the door to the market, sprinted ten feet or so towards the dock, then disappeared into a thick row of bushes.

I had a feeling that most of my afternoon was going to be spent coaxing him out from under the greenery. After twenty minutes of trying, I figured there was nothing to be done about it. I could see him and he clearly wasn't going anywhere, so I decided it was safe to leave him while I shopped. I went into the market, bought the makings for a delicious lunch – two juicy knockwurst, some German potato salad, a dark Heineken, a can of Nine Lives Turkey Giblets – then trooped back outside to assess the cat situation.

The situation was this: the cat was gone.

Standing in front of the bush he'd been hiding in, I called his name. Nothing. Not a sound, not a stirring. I got down on my hands and knees

71

and peered through the thicket, but there was no sign of grey fur anywhere. My throat felt as if I had a two-ton chunk of granite stuck in it; my stomach was flip-flopping to beat the Seven Santini Brothers. I couldn't believe it. How could I have left him alone outside? What was I thinking of? As smart as he was, he wasn't human. He wasn't even a dog. He was just a cat! A cat who'd never been outside before and I'd deserted him, left him stranded! And now he was either hiding some-where, shivering in total terror, was hopelessly lost never to be found again, or had been kidnapped by two brothers named Rick and Mick who had already tied the first firecracker to his tail.

Forcing myself to be calm, I took a deep breath and called Norton's name a second time. There was only a terrible silence. For one long second. Then two seconds . . . then . . . *brrrrrmeowww*.

A grey head with folded ears poked its way out of the bush – exactly where I'd last seen it. The rest of the body followed. Norton stood on the sidewalk, looking up at me with one of his 'What's the problem?' looks.

I didn't want him to see that I'd completely lost faith in him and panicked, so I only allowed myself a minute sigh of relief. Then I turned and walked past the market, not stopping until I was on my own front deck. There was no need to look behind me: Norton, of course, had kept pace, trotting briskly five feet behind the entire way.

Over the course of the summer, Norton's little jaunts turned into a wonderfully pleasurable routine. Cindy was having to work more and more on the weekends, so Norton was, every two or three weeks, my only beach companion. He always walked me to the market in the morning, he usually walked me there at lunchtime and he sometimes deigned to come along at dinnertime. Rarely did he walk by my side. He was most comfortable lagging those five feet behind. He would meow periodically just to let me know he was still tagging along. Once I got used to this, I stopped even bothering to turn around to check on him. I'd simply walk merrily on my way, hear him alert me that all was well, and I'd call back, 'OK, OK, let's try to keep up.' I got quite used to, as people passed us by, someone turning to a friend, whose eyes would be bugging out, and saying, 'See, I told you.'

As we both got comfortable with our walking patterns, he (and I, I suppose) got more adventurous.

My writing partner is named David Handler. We do most of our television and film scripts together; the business is so filled with sharklike monsters whose greatest pleasure is chomping their sharp teeth down on helpless writers that we feel, erroneously no doubt, there's safety in numbers. David and his girlfriend, Diana, had a house four or five blocks north of mine. On the days we worked there, Norton took to accompanying me. He got to know the route well: straight for several blocks, left, then go all the way to the bay. He got to know it so well he began making the excursion on his own. Not infrequently, Cindy and I would be cooking dinner and David would call, saying Norton had been visiting for a couple of hours but he'd just trotted away, so I should expect him home soon. Sure enough, twenty minutes later there'd be a meow at the door and a certain wandering feline would make it very clear he wouldn't mind eating a can of Cheese and Chicken Chunks and eating it *right now*.

One thing I learned early on is that I never had to worry about losing Norton along the way, no matter how far we travelled. Taking Central Walk – the erratically paved path that went for several miles along the centre of the island – to David's, Norton would periodically get distracted or frightened or simply playful. If a squirrel happened to cross his path, Norton would scamper after him, sometimes into the bushes, sometimes under someone's house, sometimes up a tree. If a dog decided to act doglike and bark or growl, Norton was out of there. Same if a bike came clanging along and cruised too close. At first I would simply wait impatiently until he'd reappear, which sometimes took as long as fifteen minutes, or I'd spend the same amount of time crawling around trying to find and catch him. Once, I was in a particular hurry. David and I were to be on the receiving end of a conference call from a producer in LA who felt he could just as easily humiliate us over the phone as in person. So I just left Norton where he'd sprinted away to, hidden under someone's deck. I went to my conference call, spent forty-five minutes trying to iron out the intricate plot elements of a super-realistic sitcom episode (involving a college student who broke out in a rash whenever the girl of his dreams kissed him), then convinced David to come and try to look for my kitten. We went to the spot where I'd last seen him, I called his name, and presto, there was Norton, popping out into the sunlight, happy to follow us back to David's, where he could spend the rest of the afternoon playing in the tall reeds by the bay.

It became obvious I could leave Norton anywhere, and for any length of time. Even if we didn't want him, he'd often follow me and Cindy when we left the house. If we were walking over to someone's place for dinner, he'd stay with us until he got bored, meow loud enough so I'd be sure to turn and see where he was, then dash off to have fun on his own. Hours later, after dessert and coffee, I'd make my way back to the spot, call his name, and with one of his *brrrrmeowwwws*, he'd be ready to head back home.

Norton clearly liked the combination of his freedom and my company as much as I did. It got to the point where it was rarely necessary to stick him into his shoulder bag/carrying case. He wanted to walk everywherc instead. Leaving for Fire Island from my apartment, he always hopped right into the bag because, even for Norton, asking him to walk on a crowded Manhattan sidewalk was a bit much. Then, when Tommy's Taxi hit the ferry dock, he'd also willingly slip off my lap or shoulder back into the bag – there was too much foot and car traffic, not to mention the general sense of hysteria from the hordes of city dwellers overly anxious to drink frozen daiquiris, get skin cancer and exchange phone numbers with members of the opposite sex who either owned or looked as if they would soon be able to own a two-bedroom co-op in a doorman building.

But once the ferry was headed across the bay, forget it. Norton was on his own.

As soon as we were seated, he was out of the bag and either on my lap or propped up against the railing, checking out the fascinating movement of the waves. He would race to the door the moment we were tied up to shore and hop onto the dock's wooden planks himself. He'd wait impatiently for me and Cindy to make our way through the crowd (Why New Yorkers line up for five minutes – on a boat! Which you can't get off because it's still in the water! – then push and shove so they can get somewhere to *relax*, I'll never know), then race ahead of us towards the house, stopping every ten or twelve feet to make sure we were following. If he was hungry, he'd deign to come inside long enough to chow down, then he'd meow or scratch the screen door until we let him out. I didn't like the idea of his staying out all night – OK, OK, so I had a *touch* of Jim Backus in *Rebel Without a Cause* in me, get off my back – and, to his credit, he always came inside when it was time for me to go to bed. Even having glimpsed the world beyond, he didn't alter our regular sleeping arrangements.

Sunday night or Monday morning, when it was time to head back to the concrete jungle, he would walk with us to the ferry, stopping right before we reached the dock, where he'd hop into the bag and allow me to carry him until we were seated on the boat.

The more comfortable I got travelling with him, the more I realized how much I could trust him.

At the ferry stop was a great divey restaurant/pub, Porky's, whose desirable fried clams were mentioned earlier. Porky's had a take-out window, and I soon got into the habit of leaving Norton's bag – with Norton in it – on one of the benches by the boat while I went to get food before boarding. (I highly recommend their toasted home-made blueberry muffins, washed down with a long-necked bottle of ice-cold Bud.) I wouldn't be gone long, maybe ten minutes, but it would usually be long enough for a small crowd to have gathered round the grey cat with folded ears who was lying nonchalantly on top of his bag, taking a snooze or checking out any interesting fellow passengers.

He was quite relaxed and extraordinarily obedient when told to stay put. Eventually, as his modes of transportation and range of travels broadened, I was able to leave him in airport lounges for as long as twenty minutes while I went magazine or upgrade shopping, and in restaurants, sitting in his own chair while I ate peacefully in mine.

One of my proudest accomplishments, leading to one of Norton's shining moments, was getting him to walk on the beach. For some reason, cats don't like the sand. Maybe it's too hot for their padded paws; maybe the water scares them; maybe they're put off by all the 'Life's a Beach' shirts, umbrellas and towels. Anyway, Norton was no exception.

Here was Norton walking along the boardwalk *towards* the beach: cocky swagger, confident gleam in the eye, the look of someone who'd been parading around town pointing his finger at a neighbour, saying things like 'Howdy, Bill, we missed you at the town hall meeting last night.'

Here he was when I'd plop him *in the middle of the beach*: cowering, shaking, racing as far away from the waves as he could get to huddle terrified against the dunes. Picture Jimmy Cagney on his way to the chair in *Angels with Dirty Faces. Norton Dies Yellow!*

I decided this simply wouldn't do.

When a kid takes horseback riding lessons and tumbles off, what's the very first thing he's told? *Get right back on*. I knew I'd never get Norton to go for a horseback ride – well, there's no point in saying *never* – but I couldn't see any reason for him to stay off the sand.

In my own defence, let me say right here and now that I'm not one of those pushy stage parents. I mean, if Ethel Merman were alive, she wouldn't play me in a musical. Although Norton is a show-quality cat, I'd never even *think* of displaying him or training him to do tricks. Those things are for *other* people. This was for me and him. He'd *enjoy* having new areas to roam and explore. Why should he limit himself when he could be frolicking with some beach bunnies down by the water's edge? To end my own defence, let me say that I felt then, and I feel now, a little too much like the parent of a nine-year-old boy who's making the poor lad take piano lessons and says, 'Believe me, he'll thank me for this when he's older.'

The first few times I let Norton loose in the sand, he was gone the moment I set him down, running for the protective safety of dirt and boardwalk. The next few times, I put him down and held him, letting him get used to the feel. He didn't struggle and he didn't appear too miserable. When I let go, he'd hesitate, realizing that perhaps this whole beach thing wasn't as terrible as he'd assumed – as I'd been telling him repeatedly – but then he'd hunker down and skulk back to real land. Not sprinting exactly but not stopping to admire the view either.

After that it got easier. His instinct was to follow me. I'd never led him astray before; there was no reason for him to believe I was starting now.

Within a week, Norton was walking comfortably on the beach, his usual five steps behind me, meowing a lot more and a lot louder than usual, but he was there. He wouldn't go all the way to the water, but he *would* walk about halfway there, wait while Cindy or I shook loose a towel to lie on, and stick around for half an hour or so, especially if he got to share any of our picnic lunch. I still believe he would have spent more time relaxing there if it wasn't for the constant *thwapp-thwapp-thwapp* of the Kadima balls.

One day, towards the end of August, Cindy and I were invited to a cookout in Seaview, one of the other beach communities. Cindy had a girlfriend who was in a 'share' there, a share being when six people split the cost of a three-bedroom house, figuring out such complicated schemes as alternate weekend visits, splitting food costs, and prorating the fee for the largest bedroom or the one with the ocean view or the one closest to the refrigerator.

On this particular weekend, all the sharers were stuffed into the house because it was the weekend of the annual Seaview Clam Bake. Every year, everyone in the small community brought food and drink to the beach – clams, lobsters, burgers, hot dogs, kegs of beer, pitchers of margaritas – dug pits for barbecuing and steaming, and cooked out, drank and generally made merry. This went on all day and a goodly portion of the night. There was usually music and volleyball games and three-legged races and other Andy Hardyish events; all in all, it was awfully hard to think of a much better way to spend a ninety-degree day in the heart of a New York summer.

Cindy went early to help prepare. She thought it would be fun to be in on the beginning of the festivities. As much as I always enjoyed the Seaview bash, my antisocial theory about large gatherings of human beings always was and is 'less is more'.

I puttered around until the late morning, did a little work, and, since Cindy wasn't around, caught up on my Rotisserie League stats. Rotisserie League, for those of you in the baseball dark ages, is sometimes called Fantasy Baseball. The game has swept the nation – *USA Today* estimates that 750,000 people now play it – and I'm proud to say I'm one of the cofounders of the original league. The premise is a simple yet immensely gratifying one. You put together a team at an auction, bidding against nine or eleven other 'owners', depending on whether you're in the National League or the American League. The structure of the team is specified: two catchers, three cornermen, five outfielders, nine pitchers, and so on. If you buy Darryl Strawberry – God forbid! – and he hits a home run for the Dodgers, he also hits one for your team. Being a total maniac about the game, I have *two* teams, which makes it nearly impossible to get any work done during the summer months. My American League team is called the Gethers YeRosebuds, my National League team is thc Smoked Fish. (I am respectfully referred to by my National League *compadres* as the Sturgeon General. And believe me, I'd way overpay if there were any way to get Steve Trout on my pitching staff.) I liked to do my stats when Cindy wasn't with me, because she thought it was rather scary that a reasonably intelligent person would actually *want* to spend two hours a day totalling up the Hits and Walks Per Inning Pitched ratio for people who toiled in such places as Memorial Stadium and Chavez Ravine.

Satisfied that the Rosebuds were sprouting up for a big stretch run and a little depressed that I saw no end to the Fish's floundering, I decided it was time to head off to the Seaview bash.

Norton was lazily sunning himself on the porch as I stepped outside. His half-ears twitched in idle curiosity when I passed him by. I think he was wondering why anyone would bother leaving such a perfect spot.

'Whaddya say,' I asked him. 'You up for a stroll?'

Now, Seaview was two miles from where we were in Fair Harbor. The only way to get there in a reasonably straight line was by walking on the beach. Norton had never gone more than about thirty feet on sand. This had the potential for disaster. But I thought Norton would like the cookout once he got there. It seemed worth a shot.

My pal was ready to give it a go. He lifted himself up from his sprawled position and began trotting after me. When it came time, half a block later, to descend to the beach, he meowed loudly.

'Come on,' I coaxed gently. 'What have you got to lose?'

If I'd been by myself, I probably would have made it to the party in twenty-five minutes. With Norton, I got there in thirty-five. He was perfect – never slowing down, never letting himself be distracted, always keeping pace right behind me, except for when he got frisky and raced ahead of me. He meowed a little more than usual, but he didn't seem to be complaining. He was just feeling gabby.

The way Seaview is set up along the beach, you have to climb up a small incline to get there. When you've climbed, you're standing on a dune overlooking the town's entire stretch of beach. It's not the Grand Canyon or anything, but it's quite nice, especially on a day when there are a couple of hundred people happily cooking and serving and playing.

I climbed, stood there for a moment enjoying the view and spotted Cindy. She waved; I waved back. I swivelled my head back behind me to check on the walking wonder and said, 'Let's do it.'

Norton meowed once and followed. Up the incline, down into the laughing hordes. Within moments, the noisiest event of the season was eerily quiet. One by one, heads turned, eating stopped, music ceased. These sophisticated Fire Islanders had seen frisbee-playing dogs in their midst. They'd seen a spider monkey with a pail and shovel digging holes in the beach. They'd even once seen a female member of the singles-oriented Kismet community who *wasn't* wearing an ankle bracelet. But they were all staring at the kitten who'd traversed the sandy shores to help them party hearty – Norton of Arabia.

'Where did you come from?' the first person I passed asked.

'Fair Harbor,' I told him.

'Your cat walked *two miles* like that?!'

I nodded. By the time I reached Cindy and her friends, I was nodding like a madman, my head bobbing up and down, and I was repeating all the familiar phrases: 'Yup, does it all the time . . . Scottish Fold. See the ears? . . . Norton . . . Two miles . . . Fair Harbor . . . Yup . . . See the ears?'

Gradually the cookout went back to normal. The band started up again, backgammon games resumed, shrimps were skewered. Norton, after sampling some grilled tuna, went to play in the grass, away from the sand. I went with him to the steps leading away from the beach, told him I'd come get him in a few hours. I picked him up, kissed the top of his head, then I watched him disappear, knowing he'd be waiting when it was time to go home.

5

The Cat Who Went to California

My Fire Island landlord was nice enough to extend our summer season until the end of September. But over the Labor Day weekend it hit me: what was I going to do with Norton when I didn't have a summer home where he could frolic the day away? How was he going to adjust to being an indoor cat? Especially – since I had recently learned that the biggest cause of fatalities in New York City cats was their leaping to their deaths out of apartment windows – an indoor cat whose father wouldn't ever again open a window so much as a crack.

By 1 October, I hadn't come up with any intelligent solutions. Norton's travels were relegated to going back and forth between Cindy's and my apartment. When she spent the night at mine, Marlowe would come along. He was perfectly comfortable at my place, so it seemed only right that Norton should be their houseguest when the sleeping arrangements were reversed.

I was starting to do a fair amount of business-related travelling. (I should probably explain that the travelling was complicated because my business was complicated. I should say business*es* – and perhaps 'confusing' is a better description than 'complicated' since I don't actually have one job, I have several, none of which makes all that much sense. One part of me runs a publishing company. That part allows me to make honest-to-goodness grown-up financial decisions, meet anyone interesting I can think of who might like to write a book, and work with very talented and very temperamental authors and personalities. Another part of me writes and produces television and movie scripts. That part allows me to wear sunglasses and hate actors and get really aggravated when producers say things to me like, 'I love it! It's perfect! And don't worry, I know exactly how to fix it!' – which actually *was* said by the executive producer of a TV series I worked on. The third and final part of me – probably my favourite part – writes books. This is the part that allows me to sit alone in a room and torture myself trying to invent characters and plots that most people will never read or hear of. It also gives me a chance to create some meaning out of all sorts of otherwise meaningless things. None of these jobs particularly fits together and

I never actually meant to turn into a compulsive workaholic – but somehow it's happened and I kind of like it.) My publishing job – at this point I was helping to start a new imprint within the large and still growing Random House complex – would take me away for a sales conference here and there, a trip to San Francisco to see agents, a quick sojourn with an author to make sure he or she felt loved and appreciated. My writing career was also keeping me busy and on the road. When you live in New York and write for Hollywood, you've constantly got to prove to the networks and studios that living three thousand miles away from the people paying you – and usually paying far too much money to write things that never get made – isn't anything they should worry about. The only proof is visibility, which meant my partner David and I had to hop on a plane on a fairly regular basis and show our faces around town.

Norton and Marlowe were great pals; thus it was never a problem figuring out what to do when I went away: Cindy would take him. She was nearly as crazy about my guy as she was about hers and she truly enjoyed watching the two cats play and stay together for three or four days in a row. All three of them had fun when I was gone.

Everything seemed perfect until this pleasant and easy routine was forced to change. Cindy broke it to me that she was having a little *too* much fun when I was gone.

We had a strange relationship, Cindy and I. I had been smitten the moment I saw her; she had hated me on sight. She thought I was smug, egotistical and watched too much baseball. But I was persistent – writing, sending flowers, calling, doing everything but watching less baseball – and eventually won her over. We couldn't have been more opposite. She was wary of relationships and hesitant to get involved, positive that she'd be wounded irreparably just at the moment she relaxed enough to decide our particular relationship was a permanent one. Although I didn't believe in or even consider the possibility of permanence, I was an incurable romantic and was more than happy to rush in with my chin jutting and get knocked out with the first straight right hand that came my way. She didn't believe in spending money unwisely and thought it was almost sinful to spend it on one's immediate pleasure and comfort. I believed in spending any money I received as soon as possible – and *only* on things that would bring me pleasure and comfort. She thought she was a terrible human being – which she most certainly was not – while I, on the other hand, couldn't imagine anyone being a better, nicer guy than me. She got depressed all the time; I was almost always happy. She was always cold; I was always hot. She thought it was important to be serious – that times were bad and only serious thought and behaviour might improve them. I was of the *Sullivan's Travels* school of behavioural thinking – times *were* bad, so let's laugh it up and try to find amusement in everything. She was searching for meaning. I hoped I'd *never* find meaning in *anything* – or I was in big trouble.

What really brought us together was the fact that we had *one* thing in common – we both wanted to stay independent.

The only thing we could agree on was that we didn't believe in a standard, old-fashioned, monogamous relationship. We didn't believe in marriage. People should stay together because they *wanted* to stay together – not because a piece of paper tells them they've made a legal commitment. We wanted to be free, unrestricted. If we felt like spending Saturday night together, fine. If we didn't, fine again. No problem. And no ties.

We never actually came out and said the words 'I love you'. We danced around it with clever phrases like, 'I really love being with you' and 'I love the way we don't have to say "I love you" and we still know how we feel about each other,' but once we realized we liked each other a whole bunch and that we didn't *have* to be in an old-fashioned relationship where we saw each other every Saturday night, we fell into a very comfortable old-fashioned relationship where we saw each other every Saturday night and generally took good care of each other. Neither one of us ever really thought about making more of a commitment than we had to make. In retrospect, it seems obvious that neither Cindy nor I truly understood the nature of commitment. Although, I realize now, I was in the process of learning. It just wasn't with Cindy.

Toward the end of the previous summer, Cindy and I had spent more time apart than usual, but

I had attributed that to Cindy's new job and the fact that she was working long and hard hours. It turns out I should have attributed it to the fact that she'd fallen in love with her doctor.

She'd switched to him sometime in the spring. I remembered that she'd mentioned how great he was – and how cute. I also remembered that sometime around the Fourth of July, she'd started saying things like 'You know, you really shouldn't eat popcorn. It tends to clog up your intestines' and 'Did you know that by the year 2020, the average doctor will spend nearly a million dollars to go to medical school? Doesn't it steam you that people think of doctors as selfish and unfeeling when they have to risk so much to do what they do?'

I'd usually say things like 'Oh yeah?' or *What?* and then not give it any thought. But I gave it a lot of thought when she told me I was getting dumped for the doc. Especially because it came right after I had invited her to England – the week's vacation was to be a present for her birthday.

'I just can't live a lie any more,' Cindy told me.

I readily agreed that she shouldn't have to live a lie, although I wished she could have lived it until after we'd been to a couple of farmhouse bed-and-breakfasts in Devon. She also wanted me to agree that it was a sad thing that it hadn't worked out between us. I managed to say that I thought it *had* been working out between us.

'No,' Cindy said. 'I don't know if you're capable of the kind of feelings that I need.'

'You mean the kind of feeling where it's OK

to dump someone who tries to do incredibly nice things for you like taking you to England?'

'No, I mean abandoning yourself to love. You're an observer,' she told me. 'I don't know if you're a participant in life.'

This stopped me short. I'd always thought I was a good participator. Granted, my idea of a good time was watching *On the Waterfront* for the sixty-second time and then calling Sports Line to find out how the Mets had done, but I'd stack my life experiences with anyone's.

'Oh, you do participate,' Cindy now said, 'but you hold back. It's as if you're waiting for something.'

'For what?'

'I don't know. For something better. Something *different*. Something you don't have. And you're holding back your true self until you find it.'

'This *is* my true self,' I tried to tell her. 'You may not like it as much as Dr Polaro's true self, but it's mine.'

'You don't understand,' she said. And with that I had to agree. I had thought Cindy and I were on the same wavelength. I'd thought we were giving each other what we both needed. I'd thought there was a bond of honesty and trust between us. I'd thought we were finally at the comfortable stage, something men and women have an awfully difficult time reaching together without being in a rest home. Obviously I'd thought wrong.

I didn't stick around for too much longer. For one thing, I was getting awfully sad. For another, considering the occasion, I was fairly certain Dr Polaro's true self would be coming over soon and I didn't particularly want to be there when it did.

It wasn't easy saying goodbye to Cindy. In a weird way, it was even harder to say goodbye to Marlowe. I'd really got to like the little guy. And with Cindy, at least I could hate her a little bit. I knew that wouldn't last, but it was some comfort at the moment. I had no reason to hate Marlowe. He'd never done anything to me but make me laugh and make me feel good. I'd even got him finally, on our next-to-last weekend in Fire Island, to go for a short walk with me and Norton. He made it almost all the way to the market. Now I picked him up and scratched his full, standing-up-straight ears. 'You can come over any time,' I told him.

Norton was surprised we were leaving so soon. Once I'd lugged him over there, he was prepared to spend the night. He meowed, a tad annoyed, when I put him back into his bag. Cindy didn't pet him or say goodbye to him. In fact, she wouldn't even look at him. I think she felt too guilty. Or else she thought that *his* true self might ask her what the hell she was doing dropping us for a guy who wouldn't eat popcorn.

The last thing Cindy said to me was, 'You won't be sad for long. You don't really love me. You don't know what love is.'

The next few weeks were a little rough. I felt funny watching *On the Waterfront* by myself on Saturday night, and Norton didn't understand why (1) he hadn't been out of the apartment at *all*, not even across town to Cindy's, and (2) if he wasn't going to be able to leave, where was his friend Marlowe to keep him company?

Most of my time was taken up working and feeling sorry for myself. I found comfort in little things: I remembered that Cindy once actually told me she thought the ending to *On the Waterfront* was *stupid* – that Brando shouldn't have had to stand up at the end for the men to go back to work; he was risking serious injury (and this was *before* the doctor). I remembered that she liked to sing the theme song to 'The Brady Bunch' when she cooked. And I realized, at last, I could now take taxis everywhere without someone trying to make me feel as if I were personally responsible for famine in Pakistan. In fact, within a day, I'd managed to make a list of things about her that so infuriated me, I had almost forgotten about going back to her to beg and plead for a second chance.

Luckily for my sanity (and the sanity of those around me), I was distracted by the need to prepare for a week-long trip to California. I kept busy making appointments, figuring out what I was going to do and say . . . It was only three days before I had to leave that it occurred to me I had to do something with Norton.

I considered calling Cindy to see if she'd still take him. I was fairly certain she would, but I didn't feel it was quite the appropriate thing to do. I didn't like the idea of her knowing I couldn't manage without her. I also had visions of Dr Polaro, whom I could no longer separate from Son of Sam when trying to imagine what he was really like, performing some strange surgical procedures on Norton's fragile and vulnerable body. So Cindy was out. I called almost everyone else I knew – and not one of them could cat-sit for the week. Either they had a cat of their own and felt it wouldn't work, or their apartment building had a strict no-pet rule, or they were allergic to cats, or they were too nervous because they knew what I'd do to them if anything happened to Norton while he was in their care. By the time I'd run through my phone book, I had two days left to come up with a plan.

The reason I was going to California was that I'd agreed to speak at a writers' conference in San Diego. I was going to spend three days there, then go to LA for the rest of the week to work, see a few people, have a few meetings and spend some time with my family. Nothing too hectic, nothing too formal, nothing too intimidating – in other words, absolutely nothing that would preclude taking an extraordinarily well-behaved and well-adjusted cat.

I got on the phone immediately. San Diego was a breeze. The conference had booked all the speakers and would-be writers into a large motel near the UCSD campus. The motel was delighted to have a cat spend a few nights in their care. I had a sudden and brand-new appreciation for the laid-back, Southern California lifestyle.

Los Angeles was more difficult, however. My regular hotel wouldn't hear of it. Out of the question. The next five hotels also wouldn't consider having Norton as a customer. But then I struck pay dirt.

The Four Seasons had just built a new hotel in LA. It was in a very convenient location, was the right price and was supposed to be terrific. This was their first week open for business.

'How big is he?' they wanted to know.

'Little,' I said. 'He's very little for a cat.'

'Over forty pounds?'

'No. I said he's a *cat*, not a *lion*. I think he weighs *six* pounds.'

'Claws?'

'Yes,' I said, then realized I should have lied my head off. 'But he never scratches anything!' I added immediately. 'And if he does, I'll happily pay for any damage.' At those last words, I rolled my eyes to the heavens and prayed if there were a god that he hadn't given the Four Seasons a decorator who had a fetish for burlap wallpaper.

'Let me check with the manager. Hold on.'

I held on, a wreck, preparing all sorts of arguments for the manager in favour of allowing cats in their rooms. I decided I was even prepared to audition him. 'How's this for a deal,' I was thinking of saying. 'I'll pay for a separate room for Norton for one night, put him in there for an hour. Then you can check him out . . .'

'Hello?'

'I'm still here,' I said quietly.

'We'd be pleased to have your cat stay with us,' the reservation clerk told me. 'What's his name, so I can add him to the guest list?'

That was the first moment I realized I might be able to survive without Cindy. If I was going to marry this wonderful woman on the other end of the phone, I *had* to survive.

The day of the flight, I was totally unprepared. I had no idea how to make a cross-continental aeroplane trip with a cat, so I was forced to improvise. I assumed that if I were doing anything wrong, some right-thinking airline employee would set me straight.

I was flying with my agent, Esther Newberg, who was also speaking at the conference. Esther happened to have two fears – flying and cats – so when I picked her up at her apartment and she saw Norton, she was ready to call the whole trip off. But Fear Number Two was eradicated by the time we reached the airport. Within thirty minutes, Esther, whose mind is about as easy to change as Attila the Hun's, decided Norton was the greatest animal she'd ever seen. She couldn't get over the way he sat on my lap and peered out the window for the entire drive.

'I'm hoping he does that on the plane, too,' I told her.

'What's he done on other flights?' she asked.

I decided I wouldn't break it to her. Esther's the nervous type.

When we got to the airport, I put Norton in his bag, slung it over my shoulder and went to check in our bags. At the ticket counter, the woman gave me a boarding pass, tagged my suitcase and sent it slithering along their conveyor belt, then looked

Norton right in the eye. She smiled at him, said nothing and returned my ticket to me.

Next we went to the security checkpoint. Esther went through with no problem. When Norton and I stepped through, I expected alarms to go off to beat the band. But no. I guess those things are a lot more sensitive to steel and explosives than to fur. All that happened was that one of the female guards patted Norton's head when he stuck it out of the bag to check out his surroundings.

When we got to the gate, I began to have serious doubts that anyone was ever going to say anything about my flying with a cat. Perhaps it was a lot more common than I thought.

Boarding, Norton snuggled down into his carrier when I showed my ticket to the stewardess. All she said was 'Seat 8C'. Not a word about you-know-who.

Esther and I took our seats, and Norton hopped out of his bag and settled onto my lap in his favourite position – lying straight along my crossed legs, head resting on my left foot. I got a blanket and laid it over him, figuring it would make it easier to hold on to him when we took off.

We saw a short film, instructing us how to correctly fasten our seat belts. (I must say, my theory is that if you're a grown-up human being who can't figure out how to fasten your seat belt, the odds are that you wouldn't have been able to make a plane reservation and actually get to the airport, which means you wouldn't be in a position to enjoy this superb cinematic experience.) Then a stewardess passed by, checking to make sure everyone had managed to understand the film and do the fastening correctly. She looked straight at my lap – upon which sat the cat – smiled, said nothing, and passed by to look at the next lap. Still no one had said a word about Norton.

For two hours, Norton sat there, the perfect gentleman, staring out the window, fascinated by his first close-up glimpse of clouds. He didn't stir; he didn't make a peep. I began to relax.

Two hours and one minute into the flight, someone finally said the very first thing about the fact that there was a cat on board. It was the head stewardess, a woman of about fifty, who had the delicate good looks of Marie Dressler and the charming personality of Nurse Ratched.

'You've got a cat!' were her exact screaming words.

I looked up from my book. Norton turned away from the window to see who was making so much commotion.

'Get him *out* of here!' she hissed.

I looked over at Esther, glanced back to the stewardess.

'Where would you like him to go?' I asked.

'I don't care!' the woman said. 'Just get him out of here!'

'Why don't you open the door,' I suggested, 'and I'll toss him out over Cleveland.'

I didn't have a moment to even admire my own calm and wit, because at this point, things accelerated. The man behind me stood up and said, 'Oh, my God! There's a cat! I'm allergic to cats! Get him out of here!' The guy started sneezing like a lunatic.

'The cat's been right here for two hours,' I said, trying to be a sane voice in the wilderness. 'What the hell are you sneezing *now* for?'

The guy couldn't answer me, unfortunately, because he was too busy sneezing, wheezing, coughing, and struggling to get out of his seat belt so he could escape from the dread cat hair. I thought of suggesting to the stewardess that they should show a short film about how to *un*fasten your seat belt but decided against it.

'Get that cat under the seat!' the woman snapped at me.

'I don't think you want me to do that,' I told her.

'Did you hear what I said?!'

'I did. But if you'll just listen for a second—'

'Put him under the seat!!'

I picked Norton – who was responding to the crisis by acting particularly docile and cute – up off my lap and put him on the floor under my seat. When I told him to 'stay', the stewardess flew into an absolute rage.

'In his box! Put him in his box!'

Now, I'm not big on public scenes. I'd place them somewhere right below walking on hot coals and sitting through Bette Midler movies on my list of least favourite experiences. But I was starting to get annoyed.

'I *can't* put him in his box. He doesn't *have* a box. That's why I told you you didn't want me to put him under the seat.'

This charming woman could not have had a stronger response if I'd said, 'I'm carrying a bomb. Give me all your money or this plane's confetti.' As far as she was concerned, I was the Salman Rushdie of passengers and she was the Ayatollah.

'What do you *mean* you don't have a box?' she demanded. At this point I realized there was no way to stop this whole thing from getting completely out of hand, so I figured what the hell and decided to go for it.

'You know those little cages that cats go into? The ones that fit under the seat? I don't *have* one of those. *That's* what I mean!'

By now, I didn't think it could get any worse. I was wrong. Esther decided to get involved.

'Look,' she said – and when Esther says 'Look' at the beginning of a sentence, the only thing that comes to mind that *might* be as scary is the moment in *The Godfather II* when Al Pacino hears that Diane Keaton has had an abortion – 'one of the other stewardesses saw the cat on his lap earlier. She didn't seem to think it was a problem.'

'Stewardess?!' The woman was now in an apoplectic fury. '*Stewardess?!!*'

Esther and I looked at each other, not sure what the problem was now. Esther, ever the forceful agent, took a stab at it. 'That's right. The other stewardess walked right by and—'

'We are not stewardesses! We are *flight attendants!*'

The next five or ten minutes is a blur. I remember giggling. Then I remember the stewardess

. . . er . . . attendant accusing me of smuggling Norton aboard. I have a vague memory of trying to explain that she was mistaken, of her telling me I was breaking the law, of me telling her to go ahead and throw me in aeroplane jail. I definitely remember Esther rising to Norton's defence and unleashing a string of expletives that would have made John Gotti blush. They didn't seem to have much effect on the Dragon Lady, though.

Other than the fact that there was a wild, untamed jungle beast running free, able at any moment to terrorize the passengers – if you believed what our attendant was saying, the flight was quickly turning into one of those disaster movies starring Helen Hayes and George Kennedy – the biggest problem seemed to be that they were about to serve us some of their scrumptious aeroplane food. Apparently, health regulations make it illegal on American planes for a pet to be out of his cage during mealtimes. Is this a great country or what? We can't lick the homeless problem, but the FAA has made damn sure that we're able to sit in really cramped little chairs and eat microwaved teriyaki chicken in peace and quiet.

We did eventually work out a compromise, which unfortunately didn't involve my being able to staple our attendant's lips together. I simply agreed to forgo the delicious meal, as did my loyal agent. In exchange, I didn't have to toss my cat out and let him parachute his way to safety. He could stay on my lap. The guy behind me could switch seats with another passenger sympathetic to my plight. And our plane could continue on to San Diego without any more hysteria.

Which is exactly what we did. Norton stared out the window, perfectly content, until we landed. Mr Allergy moved to the back of the plane and spent the rest of the trip breathing clean, cat-free air. Esther was so furious about Nurse Ratched's behaviour that she forgot to be afraid of crashing and dying; she even allowed Norton to sit on her lap for a while. The evil stewardess – on principle alone I refuse to call her an attendant – steered clear of us for the rest of the trip, even refusing to bring us coffee or little Wash 'n' Dries.

The final three hours of the trip were calm.

The hysteria didn't begin again until we landed.

By the time we got our bags, rounded up two other publishing people who needed a ride, waited on line at the rental car desk, found our car, and got directions to the conference, we'd been travelling for nine hours. This is the second lesson I learned (after the one about buying a carrier that will fit under one's seat) about transporting a cat across state lines: nine hours is too long to go without a litter box.

Four people and one cat crowded into a shiny Oldsmobile. The people immediately started grumbling about being hungry and hating Southern California. The cat uncharacteristically started meowing like a lunatic. Norton perched himself on the shelf under the rear window and howled. He kept this up for fifteen minutes or so. I think it took that long for him to realize we still had a way to go to hit the motel. But once the realization set in, he decided to do something about it.

He urinated all over the backseat.

Needless to say, this didn't go over all that well with my travelling companions. Especially because we couldn't get him to stop. I'd never seen an animal – two or four-legged – pee for quite so long.

I didn't get angry. I couldn't. It was awfully hard to blame Norton. And from the miserable way he looked, he clearly didn't like it any more than we did. He just didn't know what else to do.

As we stopped at a gas station, in a desperate attempt to clean things up, I realized that I was totally unprepared to have a cat with me for the next week. Not only didn't I have a litter box, I didn't have any litter. I also didn't have any cat food, any cat food dishes, or any little cat treats. Basically, I realized that because of my selfishness in wanting him to travel with me, I'd just put my beloved cat through a crash course of Cat Torture 101.

Norton was clearly mortified and humiliated about his public . . . ummm . . . accident. He didn't seem to understand that it wasn't his fault. He hid under the driver's seat until we pulled into the motel. And once I had let my disgruntled passengers out of the car, I took immediate action to rectify my thoughtless ways.

The first thing I did was drive to a market, where I got a large cardboard box. (I've since got *much* more sophisticated about this potentially awkward problem. I now stock up on portable, folding litter boxes, twenty at a time. Any pet store sells them; they're sturdy enough to last a week or two, and they easily slip into my briefcase or travelling bag. I can't recommend them highly enough.) I bought some litter. (Again, years later, I've now got this all down to a science: two small five-pound bags of litter easily fit into my suitcase. The moment we hit the rental car, I open up the folding litter box, rip open one of the bags and *voilà*, Norton's got everything he needs, *immediately* laid out on the floor of the backseat. There's no need to torture him for the entire drive to our final destination and it makes it a lot easier for me to drive him around town the rest of my stay. Once I get to my room, I take out a second box and tear open the second bag of litter. Not only does Norton appreciate the extra facilities, I'm sure the rental car company and the hotel are a lot happier. I know the bellboys are. The first time I thought to put a litter box in the car, I didn't have a second one. So when I checked into the hotel, a not-very-happy guy in a uniform had to lug a used cat box up to my room.) I also bought a scooper at the market so I could clean the box out, a week's worth of food and a container of cat treats.

Back at the motel, I checked in and set Norton up in fine style. Two ashtrays made perfect food and water bowls. I fed him, showed him that I was setting up his litter box next to the sink, then set him on the bed and started petting him, telling him with the utmost sincerity that he was, very possibly, the greatest animal who'd ever lived. It wasn't too long before he was purring. After half an hour, I decided it was safe to unpack. I was pretty sure I'd been forgiven.

Part of the deal with the conference was that I would spend a portion of each day critiquing manuscripts. Any student who wanted my opinion could leave fifteen to twenty-five pages for me to read; then I was to spend several hours sitting by the pool, and each of the students could spend fifteen minutes with me discussing his or her writing ability (or, at least, my educated opinion of his or her writing ability). I always like this part of every writers' conference I go to. It's always interesting to see what people are trying to write and to hear what they *think* they're trying to write. Sometimes, however, these sessions can get a bit hostile. Many editors go right for the throat and actually tell the truth. This is not a recommended course of action. Many of the student writers don't take kindly to even the remotest criticism of their precious words. One has to delicately balance truth with encouragement. It's not always easy. (Imagine trying to critique, without offending the writer, an Oklahoma dentist's true account of the hilarious world of tartar control, called *Open Wide*.) I try to be gentle since, for the most part, I'm not dealing with professionals. With a pro, an editor can actually come out and say, 'This paragraph stinks. Cut it.' The pro will usually re-examine the paragraph with an open mind and, if it does indeed stink, get rid of it, or at least rewrite it. With an amateur, such a blunt response can produce anything from tears to guns. So I try to look for positives as well as negatives. Basically, I try to give the would-be writers their money's worth.

Along the same lines, I thought I should try to give Norton *his* money's worth. As long as he'd made the trek across country, it seemed foolish to keep him cooped up in the motel room. So the day of my first pool-side sessions, I carried Norton with me, set him down by my chair, and told him to have fun for the next few hours.

As soon as he was free to go where he wanted, he took off for the far side of the hotel, where there was a lawn and bushes to prowl through. Before he rounded the corner and disappeared from sight, he meowed once, loudly. I looked up, our eyes met (I'm not making this up, I swear), he made sure I took notice of where he was, then he was gone.

A New York editor who was also teaching at the conference came over to me and asked if I knew there was a freeway on the other side of the motel. I told her I wasn't in any hurry to go anywhere, and she then told me she wasn't all that concerned with my travel plans, she was concerned that my cat was going to end up as road kill. I assured her that he was all right, that he did this kind of thing back on Fire Island all the time, and forgot about it.

I began my first session, a critique of what was supposed to be a novel but what was obviously a thinly disguised true story, about a tumultuous love affair between a young Jewish girl and an older Italian man in the 1930s. The book was poetically titled *Matzos and Spaghetti* and the author was a seventy-year-old woman named Naomi Weinblatt. My helpful comments ('The dialogue is strong, but are you really sure it has a contemporary feel to it?') were interrupted by the worried editor, who stopped by to tell me she'd just been looking for my cat and he had clearly jumped ship. She'd tried calling his name and he was nowhere to be found. Once again, I told her to relax and went back to my student, who was defending her novel by saying, 'But this really happened!'

While I was commenting on the next manuscript, a Civil War novel about a beautiful, tempestuous woman named Scarlett who was in love with a handsome, brutish rogue ('You have a good feel for the era, but it seems a bit derivative'), I heard the editor's voice calling 'Norton . . . Norton . . .' I glanced over, and sure enough, she was thrashing through the bushes near where he'd disappeared, trying to coax him out. I shook my head and went on to my next eager writer.

An hour and several manuscripts later (one science fiction novel in which computers that are really human beings create human beings who are really computers; one series of uplifting essays meant to convey the simple pleasures of life, called *Hey, It Doesn't Matter If You're Fat*; one short story by an extremely clean-cut woman named Joy about an extremely clean-cut woman named Jill who's raped by the side of a muddy road, then crawls for miles until she reaches a garbage heap, which she staggers into, buries herself in filth, then dies, wanting only to know the name of her rapist so she can forgive him – my extremely helpful insight: 'Write what you know'), my editor friend had organized a little search party. There were now four or five students crawling around the lawn screaming Norton's name, begging him to come home.

By the end of the next hour (a screenplay in which screen time mirrored *real* time – in other words, *nothing* happened; a dozen poems about everyday life, of which the only thing I remember is that the author actually rhymed 'June' with 'spoon'; and a thriller that had this for an opening line: 'The bullet creased his forehead and he felt faint, barely having the energy to remove the pin from the grenade which was hidden in his coat, which he threw at the onrushing Krauts, knocking them to hell and gone, which they deserved.' My only comment on this one was 'Did he throw the grenade or the coat at the Krauts?'), I couldn't stand watching what had now become a dragnet for Norton. It seemed that most of the San Diego community was searching the grounds for my lost cat. I have to say that although outwardly I was cool, calm and collected, inwardly I was beginning to get pretty worried. What if Southern California *wasn't* like Fire Island? What if Norton decided to *find* Fire Island and decided the freeway was his best and quickest bet? What if . . .

I decided these musings were getting me nowhere, although I was quite sure one of my students could turn the situation into a bad prose poem. I decided to find out for myself if my faith in Norton had been misplaced.

Never showing my fear, I strode over to where I'd last seen him meow and called his name once. Without even a moment's hesitation, my little grey cat leaped from the bushes and meowed excitedly, happy I'd come to rescue him from all this noise. I petted him proudly, then turned on my heels and headed up the stairs towards our second-floor room. There was nothing but silence from around the pool as Norton trotted after me, ready for his pre-cocktail nap. When I opened the door to usher him inside the building, there was a spontaneous burst of applause.

As Norton scampered inside, I wondered if it would be possible to teach him how to bow. I decided it was probably worth spending a few minutes working on it.

The rest of the conference went smoothly. Norton, depending on his mood, spent part of each day in the room snoozing and part of each day by the pool prowling. He did attend one of my seminars, spending most of it asleep on the podium, directly on top of my notes.

When the readings and seminars and lectures and pool-side sessions were over, reaction to my participation was decidedly mixed. Some people thought I was too harsh; some thought I was a welcome dose of publishing reality. I judged my chances of being invited back the following year at about fifty-fifty. The response to Norton was far more one-sided. It was quite clear he was welcome back whenever he wanted to come.

Before he could return to San Diego, however,

Norton had to be introduced to the unique town of Los Angeles.

He, Esther and I got back into our rental car and headed up the coast. Our only stop was at the first market we came to before we hit the freeway. I explained to the manager why I needed two empty boxes and he was nice enough to oblige without charging me. The trip went quickly, memorable only because Norton decided to spend half of it perched on my shoulder with his head sticking out the open front window and because Esther decided to spend *all* of it complaining about the fact that the car still smelled decidedly from our last trip with Norton.

I dropped Esther off at the Beverly Hills Hotel and I went on to the Four Seasons. The Beverly Hills is just a little too show-bizzy for my taste. It's extremely difficult to walk through the lobby or make it through a meal without hearing such charming words and phrases as 'Fuck *them* if they think I'll go for a step deal' and 'The idea is great, but the concept is way off' and 'Sure, I can get it to Dusty, but is he right for it?' All these things are usually uttered by people who would, in fact, kill for a step deal, have no idea what a great idea actually is and would be terrified if they actually heard one because then they'd have to make a decision, and could only get something to Dusty if they bumped into him on the street and began the conversation with the words, 'Excuse me, Mr Hoffman, you don't know me but . . .'

I dropped Esther off at Show Biz Central and went on over to my hotel. Still a little wary from my encounter with our flight attendant, I was much relieved to hear the desk clerk say to me, with a huge smile on her face, 'And this must be Norton.'

While he sat on the registration counter, we got checked in quickly and easily, and then we were shown to our room. I was happy and, as soon as I'd set up the litter box and ashtrays for food and water, so was my cat.

Norton quickly took a liking to LA. His only problem was at my parents' house. I should say his only problem*s*.

The first problem was an unsolvable one. My parents' house was up in the hills above Coldwater Canyon and they had coyotes roaming the countryside. Once, when the folks came home from a dinner party around midnight, two coyotes were actually standing in the driveway right in front of the garage. Luckily, the beasts were as frightened of my parents as my parents were of the beasts, and nobody was eaten. But a lot of little animals in the area *had* been eaten. The people who lived next door to my folks had an adorable little poodle. They wouldn't let the dog out at night, fearful that the coyotes would attack under the cover of darkness. But they figured it was all right to let the dog romp around during the day. One morning they let the pooch outside at 10 a.m. At noon, they went to find him – and all that was left was the head and the four paws. It was pretty gruesome.

It's difficult to feel sorry for coyotes, as they're unattractive and unappealing animals, but one has to, just a bit. There's so much construction and upheaval around Los Angeles that the coyotes have basically been displaced. Their land is gone and they have nowhere to live or hunt. They are left with little choice but to hang out around rich people's homes and go after their garbage and their pets. I tried explaining all this to Norton, but it didn't go over too well. He didn't care much about the plight of the coyotes. He only cared that he wasn't allowed to venture into the backyard, which looked incredibly inviting to him. But I decided better he be frustrated indoors than coyote food outside.

The second problem was that my parents had two Golden Retrievers who had the size and intelligence of dinosaurs. Dolly and Rewrite are as sweet as dogs can be. But being around them is like being around two of the Three Stooges. They wag their tails, and expensive crystal goes crashing to the floor. They jump up to greet you, and white linen suits are covered with muddy paw prints. Go to pet them and you spend the next minutes trying to wash several gallons of dog slobber from your hands, arms and even your neck. My parents were wild about these dogs. My father had taken to calling them his 'children', and when I called from New York to say hello, if I didn't ask about them, I was severely chastised. I was fairly sure that, by this point, Dolly and Rewrite stood to come out a little ahead of me and my brother in the will.

While I will admit to liking my four-legged 'brother' and 'sister', it was difficult for Norton to warm up to them – mostly because their favourite

112

activity was chasing him at full speed up the steps, cornering him under my bed, and barking as loud as they could possibly bark, which is about as loud as anything I've ever heard outside of a Who concert I went to in 1972.

Norton got along with the few dogs he encountered on Fire Island. He was usually cautious around them but would give them the benefit of the doubt. I wouldn't say he had any dogs as his best friends, but I had seen him on more than one occasion in my backyard, lying peacefully right next to one of my Fire Island neighbour's dogs. Dolly and Rewrite, however, were another matter. There was no peace at all when the three of them were in the same house.

The matter settled itself fairly easily. When Dolly and Rewrite were outside (the coyotes willingly stayed away when these two lummoxes were running and jumping about), Norton would come downstairs and poke around the kitchen, the den and the living room. When the dogs were let in, a gate went up, blocking them off from the upstairs part of the house. Norton would lie on the steps just above the gate, secure in the knowledge that they couldn't get to him and enjoying the fact that his presence there nearly drove them mad.

The third problem was a little more delicate.

My father absolutely loathed, hated and despised cats.

I tried everything I could think of for his first meeting with Norton. 'Don't bring him to the house,' he said. I went through my explanation that my guy was different from normal cats, that he was incredibly smart, that he wouldn't bother my father, that at some point in my life, I, too, thought that I didn't like cats, but when I met Norton that all changed. This had about as much effect on my dad as it would have had on a slab of marble. He was unmoved and simply repeated his instructions: 'Don't bring him to the house.'

I have to say a few words about my father here. He was as perfect a dad as he could have been. We were terrific pals and I don't think I could have had more respect for him. For years he was one of the top television writers in LA, and then he became, in his late fifties, one of the top television directors as well. He was a bear of a person, dominating a room with both his looks and his personality. His 'shtick' was to be gruff and cynical, and on the surface he sure was, but in fact he was the most caring and generous man I ever met in my life. He solved problems and gave advice and was usually just strict enough and unbending enough to provide the right kind of fatherly support. He certainly made plenty of mistakes in his life and his career, but his correct choices more than made up for them. Cindy, who for the first two years she knew him was totally intimidated by him, once said he was the first person she ever met who was larger than life. I always thought he was funny and smart and talented and exceedingly moral, and I enjoyed being with him and my mother as much as I enjoyed being with my closest friends. But he was still my dad and I was still his son – and as such we could, without much provocation, drive each other completely crazy.

As I was taking Norton up to the house for the first time, I had a funny feeling he was going to be another one of those crazy-driving provocations.

The only thing I can really add to the picture, as Norton is about to be introduced to the family, is a brief description of my mother, who happens to be the perfect mom. While my dad tended to bluster, my mom would stay quiet and, behind the scenes, make certain everything was really all right. She has always been the quiet strength behind the family, although she always made sure that everyone else always got all the credit.

My mother, by the time she reached the age of fifty-five, had never officially worked a day in her life. One afternoon, she was in a very 'in' restaurant – at the time – Ma Maison. She had decided that she wanted to learn how to be an expert French cook, so she asked the owner, Patrick, how she should go about it. I think she had something dilettantish in mind, such as going to France for a few weeks and taking cooking classes. Instead, Patrick told her she should go to work in the restaurant three times a week – without pay – and that in six months she'd be a great cook. That's exactly what she did. She started going in three times a week as an unpaid apprentice, and within a year, not only was she a terrific chef, she had started and was running a Ma Maison cooking school. In the twelve or so years since, she's become a queen of the LA cooking mafia, writing several respected cookbooks, working intimately with people like Wulfgang Puck and befriending people like Julia Child and Maida Heatter. The only drawback to this is that my mother is now slightly obsessed with food. I can call up and say, 'Mom, I'm a little down – I got fired from my job and my girlfriend left me and I was just run over by a truck.' The odds are Mom will sympathize for a minute or so and then say, 'Did I tell you about the crème brûlée I made last night? It was wonderful. I added some lemon and . . .' And she'll be off giving me instructions on how to make the perfect custard.

My mom is fairly unflappable. Nothing much seems to bother her, and especially as she's got more secure over the years, she always seems to take the long and sane view of things. A good way to illustrate the difference between the two parents is their reaction when they saw my first New York City apartment.

I suppose everyone who ever had pretensions of being an artist and who moved to New York has at one time lived in an apartment similar to mine. But, to be honest, that seems almost impossible. I think it's safe to assume that my apartment was the worst apartment ever built in New York City. It was on Perry Street near Seventh Avenue, right in the heart of Greenwich Village. It was a basement. I don't mean a basement apartment – I mean a basement. A good chunk of what was supposed to be the living room had no floor. It was just dirt and, without working too hard, you could poke around in it and peek down to the subway. When I took the place, there was no kitchen, no bathroom, not even a shower. There was also no light. The only two windows faced the street but were blocked by the building's enormous garbage cans. It also wasn't too well constructed. On particularly rainy or snowy nights, there was usually a pretty good chance that the elements would blow through the cracks in the walls. There is no feeling quite like coming home from a Greenwich Village bar at 2 a.m. on a snowy, icy, winter morn, crawling into bed – and finding that your sheets have been soaked through and through by snow that has been drifting into your apartment all night.

In my apartment's defence, however, it did have a great painted tin ceiling and a brick wall and a great wooden floor (the parts of it that *had* a floor). Also, it was right in the heart of the Village. *And* it was only $105 a month. Even I knew, however, that it wasn't the kind of apartment that parents love to see their child living in.

I had tried, at the time, to prepare my folks for what they were going to see when they visited New York. I found out later that for weeks beforehand, my mother had driven my father nearly mad saying things like, 'Now, remember, when you see Pete's apartment, no matter what you think about it, tell him you love it.' Nearly every minute of the day, according to my father, was taken up with her lectures about how important it was to me for them to support my lifestyle and my taste. Finally my father promised he would be on his best behaviour and tell me he approved of where I was living – no matter what it was really like.

When it came time for them to actually see it

for themselves, my mother spent the entire taxi ride downtown repeating the rules to my dad. 'Tell him it's great . . . Tell him you love it . . . Try to remember what it was like when you were young . . .' She'd been psyching herself up for so long, that when I finally heard their knock at the door and opened it to let them in, before I could say a word my mother gushed, 'Oh my God! It's lovely! It's perfect! Isn't it perfect? What a great apartment!' I had the presence of mind to say, 'Mom, don't you want to come in and *see* it first before you decide if you like it?' Embarrassed, she stepped inside. My father followed. After a two-second pause, my father, looking around in wonder, blew his promise to my mother and said, 'Holy shit. What a craphouse!'

The best description of my parents – and the difference between them – came from a director named Bill Persky, one of their friends, who, in a toast at one of their anniversary parties, said it was like 'Adolf Hitler being married to Julie Andrews.'

Adolf, Julie . . . meet Norton.

I came up to the house for dinner, Norton contentedly hanging from my shoulder in his usual bag. I knew my father had told me not to bring him, but I was sure he didn't really mean it.

My mother made an appropriate fuss when she saw him. Not a cat lover herself, she appreciated the two things that were immediately apparent – he was great looking and so sweet natured. She petted him delicately, not used to being around a feline. She relaxed when Norton nuzzled her hand with his nose. As he was nuzzling, my dad called down from upstairs, 'Is that *cat* with you?' When I called up that yes, indeed, he was, the next roar was, 'Well, make sure I don't see him when I come downstairs!'

After a little bit of confusion and a bit more arguing, we all finally agreed that it was impossible for me to arrange for my father never even to *see* Norton, but I did agree to try to keep him out of the way. First I tried to get my dad to understand how special this particular cat was, but he seemed to be the very first person able to resist Norton's charms.

Norton stared at him with his cutest look. He rolled over on his back, paws up in the air, inviting my father to scratch his belly. He tried rubbing up against my dad's leg. He tried snuggling up to him. Forget it. The man was ice. He truly didn't like cats, and Norton was a cat. There was no way this was ever going to be anything but an uneven truce between man and animal.

I dealt with this as best I could, although I was extremely disappointed. I felt bad that my dad couldn't open himself up to the special pleasures that Norton brought me. But clearly he couldn't.

After dinner, I took Norton back to the hotel, making sure he knew that it wasn't his fault my father didn't appreciate him. The next few days, I made my LA rounds, seeing agents, writers, film and TV people – a lot of people who called me 'babe', told me they loved me like family, and let me know I was 'hot'. Luckily, one agent kept me from getting a swelled head by explaining to me that it was 'easy to *get* hot. The hard part is *staying* hot.'

Sometimes Norton came in the car with me, sometimes he hung out at the hotel. When he was in the car, his new idea of fun, begun on the ride from San Diego, was to perch himself on my shoulder while I was driving and hang his head out my open window. By this time I had no fear that he might jump out. That just wasn't something Norton would do. Even in LA, where people are used to just about everything, I got a few interesting double takes as we were cruising around.

All in all, I decided that taking Norton from coast to coast was a simple thing to do, bound to get simpler as we both got more experienced. And just as I decided I could see no drawbacks to it, a major drawback occurred.

I got a call from my office. We were publishing a celebrity's autobiography. As is so often the case, the celebrity didn't really write the book; he just talked into a tape recorder and with a writer who was supposed to turn out a book that seemed as if it could only have been written by the celebrity himself. This is fairly common practice, as most celebrities, at least most actors and athletes, have a lot of trouble writing anything other than the words 'I', 'me', 'mine', or 'more'. I had thought that this particular celebrity's book was under control. The ghost writer had done a terrific job, the book was entertaining and the timing was right

– this lucky celebrity had managed to *stay* hot. But as so often happens, this famous man had got cold feet. When he read over his book one last time before we were to go to the printer, he decided that, even though he'd assured us every step of the way that he loved the book that bore his name, he couldn't *really* say all those things for the record. We'd have to cut and rewrite and drastically change things – or he wouldn't let us publish. If we tried to publish anyway, he wouldn't do any publicity, which would effectively kill any chance of selling the damn thing.

This charmer lived in Santa Barbara, just a couple of hours drive from LA. Since I was already close by, the powers that be had decided I should get in my car, head immediately up the coast and get to work. I had five whole days to completely rewrite the book so we could meet our promised publication date.

No problem.

Scratch that . . . one problem.

Since our celebrity was already bordering on hysteria, and since I was going to be staying in his home – another minor problem was that since this guy drank so much, it was thought I should be next to him twenty-four hours a day or we'd *never* get finished – I didn't know what the hell to do with Norton. My author was so deranged he could claim he was allergic to cats and throw me out of his house, killing any chance for my mission to be a success.

I could think of only one thing to do.

My mother gulped but agreed to let Norton

stay in their house for the five days I was to be in Santa Barbara.

'Do you want to . . . ummm . . . check with Dad?' I asked weakly. 'Just to be sure?'

'No,' my courageous mother said. 'I think it's better if we surprise him.'

I had to agree. So, since my dad was off at a meeting, I drove Norton over to the house as quickly as possible, left even quicker and went out to spend what I was sure would be the worst five days of my life – but which would *still* be better than being around my father when he found out he had to live with Norton for a week.

I was right. When I checked in that night, Mom told me it hadn't gone as well as she'd hoped. For my mother to make an admission like that meant that their house on Hazen Drive must have been something like Nagasaki the day of the bomb. She assured me, however, that Norton was still there – and was still welcome to stay.

When I called in the second night, the report was that Norton had spent some time on the couch in my parents' bedroom and that my father hadn't thrown him out.

The third night, I had been mentally beaten into a near stupor by the aggrieved author, so I was sure I hadn't understood correctly when I heard my mother say the words 'Your father told me he thought Norton was quite handsome – for a cat.'

The fourth night, I figured I must be getting delirious trying to rewrite fifty pages a day, because I was positive my mother told me, 'Norton slept with us last night.'

The fifth night, I was too exhausted to even call home. I finished my rewrites somewhere around five in the morning, loaded the manuscript into my suitcase and ran straight for my car. I arrived back in LA at 7 a.m.

My mother, who usually is out of bed by six every day, was already up. I kissed her hello and nervously asked after my cat. She smiled, motioned for me to be quiet, and led me up the stairs to her and my father's bedroom. There I saw one of the greatest sights I had ever been privy to.

On the bed, sound asleep under the covers, was my father. On his chest, on top of the covers, was Norton, also sound asleep. My father's arm was curled around the top of the blanket, his hand resting gently on Norton's back.

We tiptoed out of the room, and my mother told me that, during the course of each day, Norton kept trying to get closer and closer to my dad. At first my dad shooed him away. Then, as Norton refused to give up, he began to be intrigued. As soon as the poor guy weakened, Norton went in for the kill. By their fifth night together, he had my dad petting him for hours while he sat directly on his chest. They fell asleep like that. My mom told me that my dad actually kissed Norton good night.

I had a cup of coffee and waited for the two pals to wake up. Norton was glad to see me, although not nearly as glad as he should have been. All my dad talked about was what an amazing thing it was to listen to Norton purr.

'He must be happy here,' he kept saying. 'He purred the whole time.'

'I do think he likes it here,' my mother acknowledged.

The last words my dad said to me, before I drove to the airport, were, 'When are you coming out here again?'

'I guess in a month or so,' I told him. 'Why?'

He caressed Norton. 'Are you sure you don't want to leave him here until you get back?'

124

6

The Cat Who Went on Dates

When I returned from California, two significant – and not unrelated – events occurred: Norton discovered Pounce. And I rediscovered the nearly forgotten, rather distasteful yet undeniably exciting ritual of modern dating.

Pounce, for those of you who are ignorant of this nectar of the cat gods, is bite-sized morsels, perhaps the size of a Cheerio. It is serious junk food, the Reeses Peanut Butter Cup for the discerning feline. Pounce comes in small cardboard cans, each can a different colour depending on the chicken, liver, shrimp or beef flavour. I saw them sitting on a supermarket shelf one afternoon and, always on the lookout for a pleasurable experience for my grey companion, decided to bring one can home and try it out.

That night, before I went to bed, I gave two Pounce (Pounces? Pince??) to Norton, then put the can inside a kitchen cupboard. I got undressed and did some reading for work. After half an hour or so, I was ready to turn out the light. Norton wasn't in his usual position on the pillow next to me, so I called his name. As usual, he came running and jumped onto the bed. But he didn't, as usual, settle right down to go to sleep. Instead he scurried and prowled and nuzzled his nose into my face until I realized he was trying to tell me something. I felt as if I were in the middle of a 'Lassie' segment, except when I finally got up and agreed to follow Norton, he wasn't trying to tell me that Timmy was in trouble. He was trying to tell me he wanted another Pounce.

I obligingly opened the cupboard, gave him one, told him that this would not be acceptable behaviour on a regular basis, then went back to bed. In the morning, I woke up, stretched, felt for a familiar chin to scratch – but there was nothing there. Somehow – I'm sure I should be a tad nervous about how closely Norton and I are attuned to the same wavelength – I knew where he was. My instinct was confirmed when I got out of bed: Norton was sitting on my kitchen counter, staring hungrily up at the cupboard that held the Pounce, scratching pathetically at the cabinet door.

I gave him two more of the biscuits and thus began a daily ritual that goes on to this day. Every morning, before I head off to work, my last deed before I go out the door is to give Norton two or three Pounce. Every night, right before I go to bed, he gets two or three more. I have no idea what makes this stuff so appealing to him, unless it's the scrumptious sounding pregelatinized wheat feed flour or the equally delicious ferrous sulphate. But I do know that the thought of eating them drives my cat wild with desire. In between his morning and late-night snacks, Norton seems to spend an awful lot of time attempting to tunnel his way through my kitchen cabinet, trying to get to the Pounce on his own. Judging by the scratch marks on the pine, he's just about ready to give the Count of Monte Cristo a run for his money. I expect a major breakthrough in another few months, when he should either reach the cans of Pounce or the apartment on the other side of the hall.

In case you haven't yet come up with the connection between Norton's snacking habits and the title of this chapter, just start thinking of women, during this period of my life, as my Pounce.

For the first time in several years, I was unattached. It was a very strange feeling. As much as Cindy and I had fought against the concept of coupledom, there was no denying that we had been a full-fledged couple – and had been for a long time. As such, we'd fallen into our own routines and been included in the routines of others.

Our deal was that although we were not required to include the other in every little social occasion, there *were* situations that qualified as command performances. If anything particularly good or interesting came up that I knew she would enjoy (or, of course, vice versa), she (or I) had first dibs. The same if anything important, horrendously boring, or terrible popped onto our social calendars, a situation where one of us needed the other's support. On the other hand, if either one of us had a normal, everyday, run-of-the-mill occasion to attend, we were not stuck – either doing the inviting or being the invitee. If I had tickets to the opening of the new Sondheim musical, Cindy *had* to be my date. If I was invited by an actor friend who was appearing in a summer stock revival of *Six Rms Rv View*, I was free to take anyone I wanted. If Cindy had a dreadful wedding to go to that involved driving two-and-a-half hours into New Jersey, I was there. If she had her semi-boring monthly dinner with her uncle who always insisted – loudly – that people were constantly coming up to him on the street and mistaking him for Rouben Mamoulian, she was appreciative if I went, but I didn't *have* to go. It made sense at the time, and it seemed to work for us, for a while at least. (I actually went to dinner a surprising number of times with Uncle Max, but no one, while I was there anyway, ever came up to him and called him Mr Mamoulian. He liked me because I was the only person he'd ever met, other than all these alleged strangers on the street, who actually knew what Rouben Mamoulian looked like. In case you're wondering, yes, he was the spitting image.) When it *stopped* working, one of the first things to get used to, if

I didn't want to go alone, was finding a partner for special occasions. As much as Norton would have appreciated the opening night of *Cats*, I don't think he could have handled most theatrical events or very many charity dinners.

I think I handled the breakup with Cindy fairly well. The night that it happened, I went back to my apartment and had a decent cry. Norton hung out on the bed and let me pet him and hug him to my heart's content. He kept looking up at me, concerned, trying to figure out what could possibly be wrong. I guess I can't say that he ever truly figured it out, but he did purr particularly loudly for a stretch, an open invitation for me to collapse, put my head on his stomach and use him for a pillow, which I did gratefully for quite a long while.

When I finally felt like talking to a human, I called my oldest friend, Paul Eagle, in Los Angeles. Paul wasn't there, however, so I had to settle for his phone machine. I left a message, something subtle along the lines of 'Hi, it's me. Just checking in. How 'bout those Giants, huh? Rams stink. Oh, by the way, Cindy dumped me and I'm suicidal. Give me a call.'

Next on my list was my brother Eric, also in LA. The message I left on *his* phone machine was a bit more rational: 'Hey. Just calling to say I hate women. Talk to you later.'

Between the crying, the soothing purring and the emotional trauma of the day's events, I was now ready to go to sleep. In fact, I was looking forward to a night of lying in the dark for several hours, staring ahead with a ghostly stare, contemplating the meaninglessness of life, followed by a fitful period of tortured dreams. That was actually starting to seem like fun. So I turned off the lights, gave Norton one last hug and kiss, and began my suffering.

I had suffered for about a minute and a half when the phone rang. I turned on the light and picked up the receiver. It was Eric, my brother, who had cleverly detected the hysteria in my message and wanted to know what was wrong. I told him. The whole story. Repeating the thing out loud, rather than just inside my head, brought a few more tears. When I was done, Eric began to be supportive.

Now . . . understand this: my brother is a great guy and we've been close all our lives. But he lives in LA. And he's a screenwriter. *And* he's been through therapy (and, worse, acting classes). Add it all up and you get someone who *loves* to be supportive. He likes to hug and share his feelings and tell people he loves them.

Which is all very nice, I must say, except that I am *not* like this. I don't particularly like to hug anyone unless there's a chance we're going to exchange bodily fluids. I don't actually think my feelings are particularly interesting; sharing them usually is about as appealing to me as the idea of sharing Leon Spinks's dentures. Another reason I'm not wild about all this feeling sharing is that I've found most people don't really want you to share your feelings. They want to share *their* feelings and then have you tell them you feel

130

exactly the same way. In general, when it comes to feelings, I much prefer showing to telling.

Nonetheless, I was in no position to complain about my brother's support. I'd just poured my heart out to him. I could clearly take a little genuine emotional contact in return. So Eric told me he was there for me. He told me he loved me. He told me he was sorry the whole thing with Cindy had happened, but at the same time, he was glad because it gave him the opportunity to tell me he loved me, which he didn't get to do often enough. I, in turn, appreciated all the sentiments, except perhaps the last one, which I thought was going a bit far, and told him I loved him, too, which I certainly did.

After half an hour of such talk, we hung up.

I was now exhausted. All that sharing had taken a lot out of me.

The light went off, my head hit the pillow, my eyes closed. Sleep was very near.

But not near enough. The phone rang again.

It was Eric. He asked if I wanted him to come east. For support. I was genuinely touched by the offer, but I told him it wasn't necessary. I had plenty of people to share feelings with in New York if I really felt the need.

'I love you,' he said.

'I know,' I said before hanging up. 'Thanks again.'

I think I actually dozed off for a good thirty or forty seconds before the phone began ringing. It was now after 2 a.m.

'What?' I sighed into the phone.

131

'Pete,' Eric said, 'I just hope you understand that I'm here for you, totally and absolutely.'

'I understand,' I said. 'Totally and absolutely.'

'I'm just so concerned. You don't sound good.'

'Well, I'm pretty tired right now. I'll sound a lot better in the morning. After I get some sleep.'

'Are you sure?'

'Pretty sure. Sleep is what's important now.'

'I love you,' Eric said. 'I really do.'

'Good night,' I said.

This time I didn't even bother to try to fake it. I sat up in bed, lights on, stiff as a board, waiting. I didn't have long to wait.

'Yup,' I said into the phone.

It was Paul this time. He'd just got my message. He was surprised how awful I sounded and wanted to know exactly what had happened. Well, by this time, I was too exhausted and too cranky to go into much detail. Also, I'd already poured my heart out once; twice in one day was near impossible. So I told him he'd have to settle for the abbreviated version and then get the full rundown the next morning. He understood, and I gave him a short take on the breakup with Cindy: trip to England, no trip to England, evil doctor, crying, crying, purring and crying, phone call, phone call, phone call, I love you, I'm there for you, I love you, tired, the end.

Paul sympathized exactly the right amount – about fifteen seconds' worth – then said goodbye. Before I could hang up the phone, though, he managed to get in one quick 'I love you'.

I sat in bed for a minute, light still on, waiting.

I knew my friend Paul. This would be a hard situation for him to resist. After all, this was a person who, when I once called him from New York, long distance, to see if he had the number of an LA florist so I could send some Mother's Day flowers to my mother, made a big deal out of finding the right number, keeping me on hold for several minutes, then gave me the number of a pet store. When I called him back, demanding the real number and yelling at him for making me look like an idiot trying to order roses from Phil of Phil's Pet Parlor, he apologized for his sophomoric sense of humour, thumbed through the yellow pages, and gave me another number – which turned out to be a bowling alley. Running up a huge phone bill now, I called him a third time, screamed, and he swore he'd do it right – and gave me the number of a Korean massage parlour. So I was fairly certain he'd be unable to resist a follow-up call now in my moment of despair. It was too good an opportunity to waste.

I was right. In two minutes, the phone rang. Wearily, I answered it.

'Are you calling to tell me you love me?' I asked.

'How'd you know?' a woman's voice answered.

'Who is this?' I asked.

'Laurie.'

Paul's wife. She loved me as much as Eric did, she said.

But not as much as the next person, an old college friend Paul had called the moment he'd hung up on me. And that old friend didn't love me nearly as much as the next three old friends who called. When Paul finally called back to tell me that the more he thought about it, he *liked* me but *loved* Cindy, I decided that my period of mourning for Cindy was pretty much over.

I realize it seems fairly brief – one night of mourning after several years of love – but I have to say that despite the emotional upheaval, there was a certain sense of relief when the relationship ended. It was a little like being reborn, although, granted, it was like being born with an enveloping sense of sadness. To fight off that sadness, I immediately began to indulge all my single-man fantasies: I bought several boxes of Sugar Pops and Cocoa Puffs and ate bowls of the stuff for dinner – with *no* vegetables on the side. I never went *near* the Public Television channel on my TV dial and watched sports practically every waking minute. (I realized I had gone slightly over the edge when I was starting to care – deeply – about which woman was going to win the Dinah Shore Open golf tournament.) I didn't make my bed. And I left all the little post-shaving hair particles on the sink – for days on end.

Of course, eventually, other fantasies and yearnings came into play. It wasn't too long before I began scratching at the cabinet door for women.

I wasn't really looking for anything serious or substantial at this point. I was much more interested in shallow, superficial and, preferably, sweaty.

I wasn't much of a dater. People of my generation never really dated. We hung out, we did stuff, we burned banks, we took psychedelic drugs and rolled around on water beds together, but we didn't really date. This was a whole new experience and I was determined to make the most of it.

The first thing I learned was that attractive women (and here I'm going with the following somewhat limited definition: models, actresses and any woman who drives her own jeep who isn't named Gutty, Rocky, or Gertie) like to go out with writers. Not all of them, mind you. A lot of them like to go out with investment bankers or very ugly rock stars or photographers who only have first or last names, not both, but on the whole, they think writers are smart and they're attracted to smarts. This works out well because I've also observed that most writers like to go out with attractive women. In fact, going out on a limb, my own theory is that, deep down, male writers, with the possible exception of Vaclav Havel and Oscar Wilde, write *only* so they can impress women. Otherwise, why go through the sheer agony of lonely, torturous days trying to create, not to mention entire lifetimes of poverty and often ridicule? It's all done in the hope of an Ophelia, an Emma, a Daisy coming up to you in a bar and saying, 'Excuse me, aren't you Fyodor Dostoevsky? I just *loved The Brothers Karamazov*. That Alyosha was the *sexiest* man. Is it true that writers create characters based on their true selves?'

Models go for smarts, I believe, because they don't respect their own beauty. How could they? They're around women all day who are even *more* beautiful than they are. Where I see perfection, they see hair that's not as thick as Paulina's. I see sculpted grace, they see skin that's not as tight as Christie's. Their beauty has no mystery for them, no allure, because they see it as something they have no control over. It's an external, artificial attribute. Writers, on the other hand, worship beauty above all. This is partly because most of us are ugly little rodents with bad posture and ailing gums whose sole sense of worth comes from what we can produce from within. And it's partly because we spend most of our lives stooped over a word processor trying desperately to *create* beauty – and we know how difficult, how near-impossible and absolutely hellish that is to do.

So . . . it's established that writers go for attractive women and that attractive women go for writers. But there's one other thing that women tend to go for and fuss over and melt at the sight of.

Riiigghhhtttt.

Cute grey cats with round heads and folded ears.

Hallelujah.

The first step in restructuring my social life was to decide what to do about a place for the summer. The little blue house in Fair Harbor had never been *my* house as much as it had been *our* house. Cindy and I had found it together and enjoyed it together.

It didn't seem right for Norton and me to go back without her and Marlowe.

Enter Norm Stiles, a man destined to go down in the Fire Island Hall of Fame.

A friend for several years, Norm had been out to the house to visit us a few times over the various summers. Now he'd decided it was time to take the plunge and begin regular weekend visits. He asked if I wanted to share a house.

The more I thought about this, the better it seemed. It would be fun to have a big place instead of the blue doll's house. It would be great to have a regular tennis partner. We could have parties – actual people coming over to Pete's and Norm's for fun and recreation. Plus, I liked to cook and Norm said he liked to clean up.

Done.

We not only took a bigger house, we took over a familiar one. David, my writing partner, and Diana had decided it was time to settle in Connecticut, so we moved into their place. Norton certainly appreciated the convenience of this resettling, since he already knew how to get to the house from all points. His only reservation about the spot was one particular bluejay who lived around there. This bird had a thing for my cat and would fly around him, mocking him loudly, occasionally swooping down and pecking at Norton's head. Norton *hated* this bird. I used to try to explain to him that *he* was the cat, he was supposed to be able to take a bird one on one, but my pep talks never took hold. Until the day we left Fire

Island, Norton was totally intimidated by the bluejay.

My initial instincts about the move had been correct. Having a bigger house was a nice luxury. Norm and I played combative tennis. I learned to make a mean grilled chicken and Norm turned out to be the best dishwasher stacker I ever saw. (I swear, it seemed that he could cram most of the house, including the living room couch, into that thing.) But the one thing I had to get used to was people.

I'd been a summer resident of Fair Harbor for four years. In that time, I hadn't met one single person other than the two guys who ran the market, the Rockette Lady, and my excuse for not writing – the coffee klatch. A good part of this is due, as I'm sure you've realized by now, to the fact that I welcome new, close relationships into my life about as warmly as the eighteenth century welcomed lepers. Norm, on the other hand, had been a weekender for about a minute and a half before he knew every single person who had a home in the community, most of their regular guests and all of their personal habits. Walking down the street with Norm was an amazing experience. His level of popularity was such that I nicknamed him 'the Mayor', as in 'the Mayor of Fair Harbor'. Thinking of Norm as the Ed Koch of the beach set was not so farfetched.

'Hey, Norm! How's it hangin'?'

I couldn't get over the fact that near total strangers would just stop and pat him on the back. Women flocked around him. Norm happens to be the head writer for 'Sesame Street', which, in addition to being the best job in the world, means that women automatically think he's intelligent, sensitive and funny. He actually is all of those things – although if you ever meet him, ask him what he *was* doing with those binoculars on the porch that night.

'Norman, you were a wild man last night! Are you discoing tonight?'

I had to stop at this one and ask him where the hell one discoed in Fair Harbor. Norm told me they turned the restaurant into a club at 11 p.m. Shocked, I wondered when they'd started doing that, a week or two ago? No, Norm told me – four years ago.

Oh, well. So I wasn't big on staying up past ten o'clock during the summer.

One little guy who obviously *had* been out and around, however, was a certain debonair Scottish Fold.

Norton usually tagged along on my strolls with Norm to the tennis court or the market or the bay. It was unbelievable how many Fair Harborites knew him. It seemed that every other person we passed would first say hello to Norm, then give Norton a warm greeting – by name – then look at me and stare quizzically, as if to say, 'Hmmm, this guy looks vaguely familiar. Oh, well, maybe not.'

Sometimes I'd initiate the conversation and ask how they knew my cat. A common response was 'Oh, he comes over and visits with us all the time.'

When people would speak to me directly, I'd usually get 'Oh, you're the guy Norm told us about. Is it true you refuse to ever leave your porch?' or, my favourite, 'Ohhhh, you're Norton's dad!' It wasn't until *many* people had greeted Norton on our strolls that it occurred to me he never wore a name tag. Which meant that unless he *spoke* to my neighbours when he went visiting, they couldn't possibly know his name.

I decided not to pursue this line of thinking any further. It didn't seem healthy.

'Normie, meet you at the sixish ce soir?'

Now this is something that deserves to be discussed.

There was a strange and eerie Stephen Kingish ritual that took place in Fair Harbor every Friday and Saturday evening. As I'd sit on my porch sipping a beer, shoes off, relaxing, I'd see scores of people, dressed as if for the ballet – or, at worst, a 'Miami Vice' audition – parading by, heading towards the dock. Most of the women had on enough make-up to make the National Kabuki Theatre of Japan proud. Most of the men had on shirts that revealed enough hair on their chests, shoulders and backs to re-sod a good-sized minor league baseball stadium. They all had drinks in one hand, and their arms were all cocked at forty-five-degree angles, I suppose the best possible angle to prevent spillage.

It wasn't until Norm was there to explain the mysteries of Fire Island that I truly understood what I was witnessing.

The dock was the best place in town from

which to watch the beautiful sunsets. So all the townspeople would gather there under the pretence of enjoying nature's spectacle but, in reality, desperately trying to pick up any member of the opposite sex who didn't have sun poisoning and spend the night with him or her. These gatherings regularly started around six in the evening, thus the endearing word 'sixish' was born into our vocabulary.

There were regular sixishes and special sixishes (like Fourth of July, when there were not only fireworks but local artisans peddling their photographs, jewellery, T-shirts and personalized Kadima paddles), and there were theme sixishes. There was something awe-inspiring when, come the annual *Animal House* sixish, fairly successful lawyers, publishers, realtors, what have you, would stand around in togas, sipping their drinks, swivelling their heads in search of amiable companionship, and chanting, 'Par-*ty* . . . par-*ty*.'

Norm took me to a sixish, against my better judgement. I didn't really like mingling with people who dressed up in togas (even if they weren't dressed in togas then, it was enough to know that they *would* do so at some point in the summer), but he decided it was something I had to do. This was supposed to be a new life.

I brought Norton along, figuring he'd like to see it. Why not – he already knew most of the people who were there.

I have to say, I didn't quite get it. The whole concept slid right by me. Why would people come from New York City – the stress and dress capital of the world – to the most beautiful, quiet, relaxing beach imaginable and *re-create New York*? Why would anyone wear stockings on an eighty-five-degree Saturday night when they didn't have to? Or silk sport jackets? Why wouldn't people wear shorts and a T-shirt? And what was this fear of spending an evening alone? After five days of pushing and shoving your way through several million people crammed into a few square miles, why would anyone want to cram into a few square feet with several hundred of the same people?

Norton was a big hit at his first sixish – he got many compliments, from old friends as well as new, on his ears as well as his personality. I was less of a hit. No one complimented either my ears or my personality. I think I found it a little too hard to conceal my despair at the amount of exposed cellulite. It was as if I'd been suddenly transported into Jack La Lanne's personal hell. (For those of you who have already been captivated by Norm's charm and think he's a much more sensitive guy than I am, please note that after this first dockside experience of mine and ensuing state of shock, he devised the perfect sixish lure for a member of the opposite sex: first, tie a piece of Danish to a string. Any flavour will do, though cherry, prune or cheese are preferable. Casually drop said Danish on the ground. When your unsuspecting prey bends over, thinking he or she can surreptitiously shovel away some free dessert, yank the string, pulling the delectable pastry several feet closer to your house. Your prey will pursue. Repeat as long as necessary, which is until you've got the poor sucker trapped in your living room. This simple trick should be good for up to a solid three blocks. For best results, have lit candles, a batch of frozen daiquiris and some peanut M & M's all set up, waiting at home.)

Norton, to his credit, seemed to share my lack of interest in the sixish. There were certainly no other cats to befriend. The only other quadruped was a small sheepdog whose idea of fun was barking loudly and chasing Norton into the bushes by the market. We left after I overheard a conversation Norm was having with a woman psychologist. Her specialty was people with ego problems. 'Sometimes,' she was saying, 'I want to shake these people and say, "Don't you understand? I'm the best damn psychologist in New York! Why don't you just get better?"'

Norton let me carry him after that one. We both wanted to get home as quickly as possible.

Norm, Norton and I shared a summer house for three years. Norm set new records for popularity on the island and – I like to think that rooming with me was some help here – wrote some of his best sketches for Oscar the Grouch. Norton had a very happy transition from kittenhood to adolescence, acquiring all of the traits that go with the teenage and early twenties years. He became an incredible know-it-all. It was impossible to tell him anything. If it was raining and he wanted to go out, all my explanations of how he was going to be very wet and miserable if I opened the door went for naught. He insisted on learning everything for himself. He also became much more independent, taking to staying out all night when we were at the beach (or *almost* all night – he'd usually meow very loudly for me to let him in at 5 a.m.). I never questioned his whereabouts; I did give him the benefit of the doubt that he was staying away from the all-night disco. Probably the most traumatic event of this period was the removal of Norton's . . . uh . . . manhood. Although I would have loved to have a kitten fathered by him (I'll try to stay away from any grandparent comparison), everyone and anyone who ever had a cat impressed me with their vehemence about avoiding all the things that went with breeding. It was the thought of a cat (and Norton, during this thought process, became '*a* cat', not '*my* cat' or 'that cute little guy' or anything like that) spraying all over my apartment, my clothes, my work, my life that finally swayed me. I couldn't face it. So I made an appointment and took him to the vet.

Norton's vet, who has his practice down in the Village, looks exactly like Santa Claus. He's large, jolly and has long white hair and a white beard. He's a terrific doctor with a great bedside manner. When I took Norton in for this dreaded operation, I was in desperate need of that manner.

'Really,' he told me. 'It's painless. He won't feel a thing.'

'Maybe I should stay,' I said. 'I could get a cot, set it up in his room . . .'

'He doesn't have to spend the night,' Santa told me. 'You can pick him up at five.'

'Should I do anything special for him? Buy him

a soft bed? Should I get the cable guy to disconnect Channel J?'

'He'll be *fine*,' the vet said. 'This is not going to be traumatic for him.'

The vet was right. Norton handled it like a champ. I, however, was a wreck. I spent most of the day doubled over with cramps in the groin area. I was also sure that Norton would hate me when I came to pick him up. I was positive there'd be lots of resentment. I was already dreading his shrink bills.

At five sharp, I returned to the vet's and there was Norton, slightly groggy but looking none the worse for wear. Santa showed me the incision, and when the room stopped spinning around, I had to admit that it didn't look bad. He told me to make sure Norton took it easy for one night – and then the whole thing would be forgotten and he'd be completely back to normal.

He was certainly right about that. Norton showed no ill effects from the operation, neither psychological nor physical. It certainly didn't keep him from catting around all night on Fire Island. He didn't even gain weight, which I'm sure was due to his outdoor life climbing trees and prowling the Fair Harbor undergrowth.

As for me, during these house-sharing years, my tennis game improved tremendously, I progressed from grilled chicken to a superb (if I may say so myself) cold poached salmon with an aioli sauce, and we had an incredible amount of fun. But I never managed to become an habitué of the sixishes. I also never dated any egotistical psychologists; nor did I have to resort to The Mayor of Fair Harbor's Original Danish Lure.

But I did enter the full-fledged world of hemming and hawing, awkward embraces, and tentative intimacy. In fact, I did more than enter. I plunged in headfirst.

My first real post-Cindy involvement was with a woman named Sarah. Sarah and I, it would eventually turn out, had about as much in common as Madonna and the Pope. But for the first three months we went out I thought she was perfect.

To begin with the superficialities, she was absolutely stunning. She had dark hair and skin that tanned a deep, deep brown. She had long, perfectly tapered legs and – remember, I warned you this was during my Shallow Period – she wore the shortest skirts I'd ever seen this side of the Twiggy era. She was sensuous and sensual, and to top it all off, as I got to discover when she decided she could trust me, she didn't mind doing a certain amount of her clothes shopping at Victoria's Secret.

Unfortunately, after beginning with the super-ficialities, I couldn't come up with anything else. And what kept poking through and causing serious trouble was that there were two areas in which we could never resolve our differences. One was *sense of humour*. Sarah's philosophy – which she happened to mention fairly often – was that 'A sense of humour is fine, but there are certain times in life that are inappropriate for humour.' She would get rather upset when I would unleash *my* philosophy of life, which was that she was probably right but that 'I just haven't ever found any of those times yet.'

The other great area for our fights was none other than Norton. Sarah was terribly jealous of him, most specifically because I often used him as an excuse not to spend the night at her apartment. She used to insist that Norton was my means of avoiding commitment. I suppose, if forced to analyse it, she was right, though I prefer to think he was just my means of not having to actually *tell* Sarah I was avoiding commitment. My excuse for not spending the whole night in her apartment was that I didn't like leaving Norton alone.

'He'll survive a night alone,' she'd say.

'I know,' I'd say back. 'But he won't *like* it.'

As far as excuses went, this one was mostly true. I *didn't* like leaving him alone. But there were other reasons, too. I also didn't like Sarah's apartment. It was one of those new, white brick buildings that have the same sense of warmth as Stalin's Russia. She had filled the apartment up with little knick-knacks and kinetic sculptures and modern art prints. It looked like the kind of place I always figured Andy Warhol would go to die.

We once had a huge fight when, at two in the morning, I slipped out of bed and told her I was going home. She was furious. I told her about my Norton and the Predator Theory. She became even more furious. As I kept trying to explain away my leaving, Sarah finally burst into tears and told me she absolutely couldn't see me any more. She was ending the relationship. A little surprised at the extent of her reaction, I wanted to know exactly why she felt this way.

'Because Norton is just a cat,' she sniffled. 'And he only has cat feelings. I'm a person. I have *people* feelings. But you don't care about my feelings. You really don't.' By this time she was crying heavily. 'I think you like your cat better than you like me,' she said through her tears.

'Sarah, that's just not true,' I said.

'What isn't?' she asked hopefully.

'I don't think Norton only has cat feelings.'

Needless to say, this turned out to be one of those inappropriate times for humour. Sarah wouldn't see me for two months after that.

Sarah was constantly refusing to see me for two months or announcing that our relationship was over. Somehow, though, we'd always get back together. Our reunions usually came about when we'd run into each other at a restaurant and realize we liked each other better than the person we were with, or when she'd be depressed about her job and need someone to talk to, or when I'd get the new Victoria's Secret catalogue in the mail and happen to be browsing through it at bedtime. We couldn't seem to stay together and we couldn't seem to stay apart.

One Valentine's Day, on the spur of the moment, I decided to take her up to Vermont for a weekend of skiing and romance. Sarah was so appreciative of gestures like this it was a little scary. We rarely took vacations or trips together. Again, chalk this up to that lack of a commitment.

Once, we almost went to Arizona for a few days at the Phoenix Biltmore, just about my favourite place in America outside of the Liberace Museum in Vegas. But the Biltmore refused to accept cats so, outraged, I cancelled the reservation. As soon as I did that, Sarah cancelled me for three weeks. Now, with the promise of a long, snowy weekend ahead of us, I don't think I'd ever seen her so pleased and affectionate. Even I felt a little guilty when I realized that all I had to do was, on two days' notice, find a romantic Vermont inn that took cats.

By my twentieth phone call, Sarah was a lot less pleased and substantially less affectionate. As I made my twenty-first call, I was a desperate man. When the innkeeper answered, I went through my by-now rehearsed Norton pitch. I sensed a hesitation on her part – which was far better than the immediate turndowns I'd received already – so I really poured it on. I was almost ready to go the whole route – and tell her about the time Norton rescued my poor lost grandmother in that horrible snowstorm – when the innkeeper cracked.

Which is how my Scottish Fold came to go cross-country skiing.

The day after we arrived at the inn, Sarah told me she was pretty good at downhill but had never gone cross country. We set out to remedy this. First, however, we thought we'd experiment with Norton and snow. He'd never been outside in snow before; most of his outdoor experience up to this point was in the summertime. But in Vermont, summertime was a distant memory.

There was a foot-high blanket of soft powder, so we gently tossed Norton out the front door of the inn and waited with bated breath.

The first thing that happened was that he sank without a trace. He was so light and the snow was so high and so soft, Norton was simply enveloped. In the next moment, however, he went flying up into the air, so caked with white flakes he easily could have fitted in with Siegfried's and Roy's act.

Much to my surprise, he loved the snow. He ran to the nearest tree, raced up halfway and dove back to the ground. He burrowed, gopherlike, forging a tunnel with his nose and face. He rolled over on his back, now-white paws clawing at the blue sky. I don't think I'd ever seen an animal having so much fun.

After half an hour of this, I think it got too cold for him. He showed up at the inn, snowflakes and tiny icicles dripping off his coat. I wrapped him up in a towel, dried him off, which he seemed to appreciate, and then he lay down in front of the living-room fire for a nap. By this time, of course, the owner of the inn was ready to adopt Norton as one of her own.

After lunch, Sarah and I put on cross-country skis and headed out. Norton, as usual when I went for a walk in the country, followed. I tried to talk him out of this one, but he insisted. Snow or no snow, cold or no cold, he was ready to explore.

When we hit the nearby woods, Norton didn't exactly stay on the trail with us. He zigzagged around like a lunatic, jumping onto trees, bounding into snowbanks, then suddenly stopping and meowing like crazy until I'd come and carry him for a while.

All in all, he was happy. And he was even happier when, two hours later, we repeated the towelling and fireplace routine. Even Sarah was happy and had to admit – over a late-night cognac and backgammon – that Norton was a worthwhile addition to the Valentine's Day weekend. She sighed contentedly and told me she thought she was falling in love.

Two days later, however, when I refused to spend the night at her apartment, she decided she never wanted to see me again.

In between the various romantic interludes with Sarah, there were other romantic (and not so romantic) interludes. Norton managed to involve himself in almost all of them.

For about six weeks, I fell head over heels for a woman sportswriter who lived in Boston. This meant some serious weekend commuting, either to Boston or to some college basketball game in some southern town where lox and bagels were only a disturbing myth.

The first time I went to Boston to see her, I showed up with two steaks, a bottle of red wine and a cat.

Norton liked Boston (the Pan Am Shuttle stewardesses, er, flight attendants, are *very* nice to small, friendly animals), but the sportswriter couldn't envisage interviewing Dean Smith with a cat on her shoulder, so that cooled off fairly quickly.

I went out with an editor at a rival publishing company who used the word 'Dickensian' more than anyone I'd ever met. When she was introduced to Norton, she admired his looks but made the mistake of asking if I'd named him after Norton Simon. The idea that someone thought I could actually name my cat after the world's dullest billionaire was a staggering concept to me. If she'd said Kenny Norton even, she might have stuck around for a reasonable period of time. As it was, we lasted two weeks.

One week was spent in the company of a fashion designer. She probably wouldn't have made it through the whole week except that we met a few days before Halloween and she confessed to me over our first lunch that the previous Halloween she'd gone to a costume party completely naked – except for one coat of body paint. The reason she didn't last longer than a week was that she had a tattoo of a snake on her shoulder, and Norton kept leaping at it in the middle of the night, doing his best to remove it from her skin. For some reason, she felt this a sufficient reason to end our brief fling.

One of the best things about dating was watching Norton's reactions to the women I brought home (or, in the case of the sportswriter, brought him to). Most of them he liked. The normal routine was as follows: I'd come home after dinner, usher the woman into my apartment. Norton would get a late-night Pounce; I'd introduce them. We'd go through the 'Oh, what funny ears' exchange, while Norton sized her up. If he liked her, he'd nuzzle up to her with the side of his head, pushing it against her quite seductively. This was a considerable help in encouraging my date to think more seriously about my charms.

As she and I sat on the sofa, listening to music, talking, trying to figure out what the rest of the evening had in store for us, Norton – again, only if he approved – would sit a few feet away, turn over on his back and peer up at us. This was so startlingly cute that once eye contact was made between date and cat, almost all female reservations could be overcome.

Of course, if Norton *didn't* like someone, forget it. No cute nuzzling or adorable backward glances. Oh no. In these cases we got a lot of running around, scratching at the legs of the couch (and sometimes of the woman), possibly even a little throwing up. We usually had the same taste in women, Norton and I, so when his behaviour turned, it was hard for me to get annoyed. In fact, except for the couch scratching, I often felt like joining him.

Cindy and Norton had adjusted expertly to a mutually agreeable sleeping arrangement. None of her successors were ever able to work things out quite as smoothly. (Particularly one named Michelle, who would wake up every hour on the hour, sputtering, gasping for breath and waving her arms wildly because Norton kept putting his tail in her mouth.) Norton, unlike his dad, was extremely fussy about whom he'd let scritch him under the chin in the morning.

I tended to trust Norton's judgement when it came to women, and for the most part, he gave me the benefit of the doubt. The only time we ever had a serious disagreement was over Karyn.

Karyn was a Danish model whom we met in Paris (on one of Norton's first trips). She was twenty-two years old, six feet tall, and the most gorgeous woman I'd ever talked to without actually drooling. She also spoke and read many languages, was overwhelmingly sophisticated, had a sharp and nasty sense of humour and . . . I suppose you're getting the picture that I was smitten upon first meeting. Miraculously, she was smitten, too. Life seemed perfect.

Except for one problem.

A certain member of my family decided that he absolutely couldn't stand this tall blonde woman who occasionally took up his side of the bed. Norton hated her.

My cat doesn't hiss – but he hissed at Karyn. My cat doesn't bite – but he bit her. He liked to wait until she was sound asleep and then he'd jump on her pillow and meow as loudly as he could, scaring her to death. He once urinated in her shoe – just as she was rushing off on a modelling assignment.

I tried to convince him he was wrong. I also tried to convince Karyn that I couldn't leave him in New York when I came over for a brief Parisian stint. I had no luck convincing either one of them.

Happily I never had to choose between them.

It is probably a sickness, I know, but in a choice between someone who could have won the Miss Universe contest (and probably performed some sort of simple brain surgery as her talent) and a temperamental Scottish Fold, my little cat would have won hands down. I might have killed him – but he would have won. Before it came to that, however, I learned once and for all to abide by Norton's judgement when it comes to women.

On my first date with Karyn – which lasted a week – we had a spectacular time. We ate at little, out-of-the-way Parisian restaurants, we drank great wine, I sampled my first peach champagne, we danced cheek to cheek, we held hands in underground *caveaux de jazz*. Then I came back to New York. We wrote letters, we ran up phone bills that rivalled the national debt, we made plans to meet in all kinds of exotic places.

The second stretch of time we spent together was also fantastic. It lasted only five days, which was how long I was able to get away for. That trip, two friends, Nancy and Ziggy Alderman, happened to be in Paris. Nancy, who is extremely attractive but five-feet-four with dark, curly hair, was a little thrown when she strolled into my room at the Tremoille for a glass of champagne, only to find a blonde goddess – wearing something not much bigger than Captain Hook's eye patch for an outfit – busy pouring the bubbly for us all. Zig, in one of his suaver moments, panicked completely at the sight of Karyn and told us he just had to step into the bathroom for a moment. His only error was that

he stepped into the closet – and was so embarrassed, he *stayed* there for a good five minutes,
hoping somehow that we might not notice.

The next trip to Paris, Karyn and I went out
to dinner to celebrate my first night back and our
love-starved reunion. I hadn't seen her in several
months. She looked as lovely and inviting as ever
– and Norton hissed just as loudly as ever when
she came to the hotel.

When dinner was over, we strolled back along
the streets of Les Halles, holding hands, kissing
adoringly every few steps. We arrived back at
the Tremoille and went upstairs. I prepared for
an evening of extraordinary passion. Then she
mentioned, 'Oh, by the way, my boyfriend is a
little bit upset that I've been seeing you.'

It's amazing how that kind of line puts a damper
on extraordinary passion.

'Wh-what do you mean, your boyfriend?' I
asked. 'You told me you'd broken up with him
a long time ago.'

She looked at me, confused. 'Broken up?'

'Yeah. That first time we went out . . . when
we spent a week together . . . you told me you'd
just ended your relationship and . . .'

'Oh, *that*,' she said. 'I just had to wait until he
went out of town. He was gone that whole week.
I didn't really break it off with him.'

'What about the last time I was here?'

'He was gone, too.'

'Well, why didn't you *tell* me?!'

'Because I thought you wouldn't see me.'

I started pacing around the room. I wouldn't

156

look at Norton because I was sure he'd be smirking.

'What's his name?' I asked. 'Your boyfriend.'

'Robert.'

'What does he do?'

'He's a podiatrist.'

If he'd been a race car driver or perhaps an international clothing designer, I probably could have settled for some kind of sophisticated if painful sharing arrangement. At least I could have salvaged some pride. But a podiatrist?!

'How . . . um . . . how does Robert know that we've been seeing each other?' I asked.

'Oh, I had to tell him this time, since he's in town.'

'And what did he say?'

'Robert has a very bad temper,' Karyn said with a shrug.

'What did he *say*?'

'Something about killing you.'

'Does Robert also have a very good sense of humour?' I wanted to know.

'Robert has *no* sense of humour,' Karyn told me.

That was the end of Karyn. It turned out that Robert really *didn't* have a sense of humour and really *did* want to kill me. He had some Arab blood in him, and it seemed that killing was an acceptable solution in whatever country that blood came from. Even if he wasn't actually going to murder me, I must say some very unpleasant images – my being strapped in a chair, shoes off, podiatric instruments of torture being put to good use – did flash through my mind. I had no intention of spending my life with no feet, even for a beautiful Danish model.

Norton, to his credit, never gloated. I have deliberately never taken him to Denmark, however, and I doubt I ever will. The last I heard of Karyn, she'd moved to Rome and was living with some count. I can only hope it's Dracula.

One of Norton's regular trips was a yearly jaunt down to baseball's spring training in Florida. I went every year in March with the nine other guys from the Rotisserie League. Originally it was men only and some serious baseball was watched. Gradually, wives and girlfriends were added; then, as we all got a little older, golf somehow became part of the trip. Over the years, as we wrote about our outing in our annual Rotisserie League book, players from other leagues would show up. Now it's turned into something of a big deal – a Rotisserie League convention with a few hundred stat-crazed fans coming from all over the country to watch and talk baseball with us.

The Rotiss weekend isn't for the casual girl-friend. Sarah made it one year (and managed to sell more Rotisserie League T-shirts than anyone ever imagined possible; she looked a *lot* better in one of them than any of us did), but this weekend usually fell during a period when she wasn't talking to me. So for a couple of years, Norton was my only companion. He loved the hotel we all stayed at, the Belleview Biltmore, an absolutely spectacular turn-of-the-century sprawling monster with all the

158

old Southern charm one could want. Part of that charm was that the people who worked at the hotel loved Norton as well.

The second year that Norton went with me, I also took two married friends, the same ones who met Karyn in Paris, Nancy and Ziggy Alderman. (Ziggy is not his real name. His real name is John, but because he works at a rather strait-laced investment brokerage, he doesn't want them to know that to most people he's something out of a David Bowie album – which makes it somewhat complicated being friends with him. When he's with his officemates, we're supposed to call him John, even though they call him Aldy. As if that's not confusing enough, there's another hotshot named John at the firm, a hotshot with more seniority than Ziggy, so Zig's bosses told him they were going to refer to him as Jack to avoid confusion when people in the office yelled out for John. As a result, some people now know him as Ziggy, some as Aldy, some as John and some as Jack. It's a lot like being friends with Sybil.)

On the way down to St Petersburg with the Aldermans (or, if you prefer, Alderpeople), Ziggy/John/Aldy/Jack was giving me a very hard time about my bringing Norton. He couldn't understand how I could lug a cat along to such a macho affair as a spring training trip. I was made an object of ridicule for the entire flight – something my pal Zig is an expert at. Several years ago, the three of us went out to the Arizona Biltmore for five days of tennis and golf (right – Sarah wasn't speaking to me that week). The second day we were there, three friends of mine came down from Tuscon for a meal. We all ate a lot and drank a lot at the fairly expensive hotel dining room. When we were all done, Ziggy insisted on picking up the check. I argued with him – these were my friends after all; he'd never even met them before – but to no avail. He signed the bill with a flourish and basked in our profuse thank-yous the rest of the night. For the next two days, overcome by guilt, I did my best to pay for everything – Nancy's and Zig's breakfast before we played golf, the round of golf itself, drinks at the nineteenth hole, you name it. When it came time to check out, as I was handed my bill, Nancy said to her hubby, 'Don't you think it's time to tell him?' It was – and Zig broke it to me that he had indeed signed for the big dinner check – only he'd signed *my name*.

Anyway, the expression on his face as we stood in our Florida hotel's lobby didn't make up for the near-millions he'd stuck me with in Arizona, but almost. After hours of tormenting me for bringing my cat, Zig had to stand at the check-in desk and watch every attractive woman who worked in the hotel (no more than ten or fifteen of them) screech, 'Norton? Is that *Norton*?' Then he had to watch them come over, play with you-know-who, smile at me, and say, 'Remember – if you need anything, just call.'

Now that I think about it, it *did* make up for the check.

The annual Rotisserie convention was also the site of perhaps Norton's greatest adventure.

A couple of years ago, I went down as usual to

160

do my Rotisserie scouting. Also as usual, Norton came along. My plane was quite late, so we didn't arrive at the hotel till after 8 p.m. After the celebratory greeting of Norton at the desk, I put him in our room on the second floor, set up his food and litter box, then went downstairs for dinner. After a couple of hours of decent food, good beer and excellent baseball chatter, I was exhausted, so I went back up to the room. The rest of the gang went to the outdoor patio restaurant for more of the big three.

This year, I had a balcony off the bedroom. When I entered, Norton was standing by the balcony door, anxious to be let out. He was used to having the run of the Belleview Biltmore. They have a huge pool area with lots of grass and many bushes for him to skulk around in. His favourite part of the hotel, for some reason, is the basement. He has spent many a day wandering its nooks and crannies; he particularly likes one dusty concrete corner; it seems to be the perfect napping spot. But he'd never, at least to my knowledge, played up on the various steeples and levels of the roof.

After a moment's deliberation, I figured I'd give it a try. What could go wrong? So I opened the door. Norton scooted onto the balcony, hopped up on the railing and then went over, exploring the peaked roofs that seemed to stretch for miles. I waited ten or fifteen minutes, called out for him as a test, and sure enough, he came running. That let me know it was safe, so I told him he was free to roam.

Forty-five minutes later, I was ready for sleep.

As I stepped over towards the balcony to call Norton in for the night, my phone rang. I picked it up to hear the voice of Glen Waggoner, an original Rotisserian and one of my best friends.

'I think you'd better come down here.'

'What's going on?'

'Norton just fell through the roof of the dining room.'

You know the cartoon of the Road Runner, zipping along the road, covering many miles in mere seconds? That was me racing down the stairs to find my cat.

When I got to the patio, the Rotiss group was hysterical with laughter. Glen led me over to the middle of the dining area and pointed up. Ten feet above my head was a gaping hole in the green-and-white striped awning. Apparently, Norton, bored with the roof, had crawled out onto the awning. Midway, he reached a weak spot and the thing gave out. He plummeted sixteen feet down, landing inches from a table where two seventy-year-old women were finishing their dinner. Needless to say, they screamed – you'd scream, too, if you were calmly eating in a restaurant and a cat came flying through the air, landing three inches from your head – and one of them came very close to needing CPR. They were very nice about it, however, as I began apologizing (over the background din of an entire Rotisserie League crying with laughter), and they suggested I find my cat, as doubtless he was far more terrified than they were.

Glen, whom Norton knew well, had tried to

catch him after the great fall, but Norton wouldn't be caught. He'd gone racing around in the dark until Glen lost sight of him.

Having no idea where he'd run off to, I stumbled around the giant lawn, calling out his name. No response. I kept stumbling for fifteen or twenty minutes with no sign of Norton, until I suddenly realized where he had to have disappeared to. I went over to the creaky, wooden basement door, opened it and stepped inside. My eyes took a few minutes to adjust to the pitch dark; then, when they had, I inched my way towards a familiar, dusty corner. There, sound asleep, was Norton.

'Pssst,' I said.

Norton's eyes opened; he *brrrmeowed* and came into my open arms.

For the rest of the weekend, people fussed and clucked over him. But he stayed close to me for the remainder of our stay. He'd had enough adventure. I saw him nuzzling up to only one person who worked at the hotel – a very attractive blonde woman who worked at the desk. When I went over to get the little troublemaker, the woman smiled at him, then at me.

'Is he yours?' she asked, practically batting her eyes. 'He's so *sweet*.'

If I didn't know better, I'd swear that Norton winked at both of us.

7

The Cat Who Went to Paris

Over the course of Norton's first few years on earth and in my care, he had, for the average cat, led quite an exciting existence. He'd been lugged around the streets of Manhattan in a pocket. He'd taken cab rides and boat rides and train rides. He'd explored the beaches of Fire Island, the snowy peaks of Vermont, and the antiques stores of Bucks County, Pennsylvania (a trip that was relatively uneventful, except for the fact that I bought a beautiful eighteenth-century maple cradle that became Norton's favourite and nearly unbearably cute place in which to nap). He'd also become a regular at my office – spending the day with me on the average of once a week – and as soon as that was established as normal behaviour, he began coming to company sales conferences. As a corporate guest, he'd been to Phoenix, Arizona; Laguna Beach, California; Bermuda; and various places in Florida. Basically, if the trip was no more than an hour or two on the plane, he came with me no matter how long or short my stay was going to be, even if it was an overnight trip. If it was a cross-country expedition or something else that could turn out to be gruelling for him (e.g., more than five hours without a litter box), then I wouldn't take Norton unless I was going to be away for at least five or six days.

One of my fantasies in my pre-Norton days was to have a dog that I could one day take to France. The French love animals; they treat them a lot better than they treat tourists. Even the fanciest restaurants allow dogs to come and make themselves at home during mealtime. It is not uncommon to see tuxedoed gentlemen and fur-clad society ladies dining in Jamin or Rovuchon or L'Ambroisie with their poodles or their dachshunds lounging under the table. Several years ago, a French publisher put out a restaurant guide rating every restaurant in Paris by how they treated dogs: what kind of scraps they gave them, whether they were allowed in leashless or not, how friendly the waiters were when petting was called for.

It had never actually occurred to me to take Norton overseas. I'm not sure why there was this mental lapse. Perhaps it was simply that in the first few years I had him, I wasn't making a lot of European trips.

That all certainly changed in a hurry.

The change came when I got a phone call from Roman Polanski.

'Peter,' he said in his distinctive accent that combines a bit of Polish rebel, French intellectual, English dandy, American rogue and Jewish uncle, 'have you ever seen Paris at Christmastime?'

Roman and I first worked together in 1982, on his autobiography, *Roman by Polanski*. We'd worked extremely well together and, for some unknown reason, immediately became fast friends. I know he's been surrounded by controversy for most of his life, but to tell you the truth, I've never seen a particularly controversial side to him. We thought alike on a lot of issues, shared the same sense of curiosity combined with approximately the same amount of cynicism. From a friend's point of view, he happens to be an extraordinarily generous guy – there's nothing he won't do for you if he likes you – and he has a great sense of humour. He tells wonderful stories and likes nothing better than to sit around La Coupole, sipping champagne, slurping raw oysters and swapping good jokes.

I have met a lot of very, very smart people, but Polanski is probably the only genius I know. He speaks something like twelve languages, has one of the most interesting interpretive minds I've ever encountered, has made some of the finest, most original films of modern times, and, to top it all off, knows somewhere in the vicinity of a million long-legged models named Suzette. All of this is to say he doesn't ask questions like 'Have you ever seen Paris at Christmastime?' without having something in mind.

'Uh . . . no,' I said, cleverly. 'I don't think I have.'

'It's very beautiful. Very beautiful. The snow comes down, the lights go up. Ohhh, the lights in Paris, mmmmm, magnificent. It makes you cry. And the women . . . there is a tremendous influx of attractive women at Christmas, Peter.'

'Can I ask you one question, Roman?' I asked from my New York City apartment.

'Anything. Anything.'

'Why are you telling me all this?'

'How would you like to come to Paris for Christmas and help me write my new movie for Harrison Ford?'

The man has style, *non*?

Of course, I played hard to get. No pushover am I. I told him that it would take me at least four or five seconds to pack and catch a plane out of New York. It actually took me a little longer than that – but not much. Within a week, Norton and I were on our way to Europe.

Many people think that taking an animal overseas is some kind of major deal. A lot of them think there's a quarantine (only in England) or that the travel arrangements are extraordinarily complicated or that hotel accommodations are impossible for pets. The truth is nothing could be easier than lugging one's cat to foreign shores – if you do it right. Naturally, the first time I took Norton I did it all wrong.

Polanski was going to be in Amsterdam to promote his newest film. As I was making my – excuse me, *our* – arrangements, he said, 'Peter, why don't you fly to Amsterdam? We'll have a great dinner, do our best to get in some trouble, and then go to work the next day in Paris. Amsterdam is the perfect place to recuperate from jet lag.'

Makes sense, doesn't it? It certainly did to me. So as a result, Norton's first European stop – after a one-hour layover at Charles de Gaulle airport – was Amsterdam.

Before we left, I had to take my pal to the vet so he could get his cat passport. This procedure was quite simple: the vet gave Norton a shot, swabbed his ears out with a Q-tip, looked down his throat, then filled out a small green card saying that Norton Gethers, an eight-pound Scottish Fold, born in Los Angeles but living in New York, was healthy and able to change continents at his owner's discretion.

The flight was a breeze – with one tiny exception. Norton had been on a number of flights on various American airlines. As a result of their rigidity, I was a strict rule follower. I usually put Norton in his box, kept him under the seat for the whole flight, and only dared to bring him up and out onto my lap if a – OK, I can say it now – flight attendant asked to see him, which didn't happen all that often. But on Air France, Norton was greeted as warmly as if he'd paid full fare. The attendants *loved* having a pet on board and immediately told me to take him out of the confining box and make him comfortable. We were flying first class, thanks to Warner Brothers, and we were both treated in a first-class manner all the way down the line. When I was served champagne and caviar, Norton got a little dish of smoked salmon with a cup of milk. At dessert time, I mentioned that Norton had a weakness for chocolate and, *voilà*, his own personal *mousse au chocolat* arrived *tout de suite*. They were so incredibly nice to my travelling companion that I relaxed. I relaxed so much that about two hours over the Atlantic, with Norton resting contentedly on my lap, I fell sound asleep. I would have slept all the way to Holland except for the fact that, at some point, one of the male attendants gently poked me in the shoulder, waking me up. When I rubbed my eyes and oriented myself, I realized that there was no cat on my lap. When I looked up, I saw that that was because the attendant was holding him by the scruff of his little grey neck. Horrified, I grabbed Norton, put him back on my knee, and began apologizing to the steward. I was so intimidated by the strictness of American stewardesses, I apologized profusely for a good five minutes before I realized the kindly French steward was saying to me, 'Eet's all right. We don't mind. 'E was 'aving a goot walk.' Eventually I came to understand that the steward really *didn't* mind. So I got up the nerve to ask the one question I really wanted an answer to: 'Where did he go?'

At that, the steward crinkled up his nose disapprovingly. Clearly Norton had done something that this man found repugnant. In fact, by French standards, my cat had committed the ultimate sin.

''E was back in toureest,' the steward told me with disdain, 'talking to a *dog.*'

I stayed awake the rest of the trip. Norton spent most of his free time staring out the window, down at the Atlantic. He seemed to find it just as fascinating as the Fire Island Bay.

When we landed in Amsterdam, we took a cab to what turned out to be a wonderful hotel, the Amstel. I was all prepared to either hide Norton or lie my head off, claiming that he wasn't actually spending the night there, I was merely dropping him off to some Dutch friend. But there was no need for the cloak-and-dagger routine. The woman who checked us in gave the cat a warm smile, told me to take him out of his bag, and then watched with an amused look as Norton plopped himself down on the counter and made himself at home. The manager of the hotel came over immediately to get in a few friendly pats on Norton's head; so did a couple of bellboys. The check-in woman asked if Norton was indeed staying there for the night, and when I nodded hesitantly, she immediately asked if he would like a small plate of fish. I sensed that Norton's ears, what there were of them, pricked up a bit at the word 'fish', so I told her that would be very nice.

Up in the room, I set up Norton's first international cat litter box, waited for his fish to arrive, then called Roman. After a quick nap, I was ready to go.

Norton was content to spend his first night in Europe sleeping on our down bed while I was wined and dined at a spectacular Indonesian restaurant by a few Dutch journalists. (OK, Roman was the one being wined and dined – but they let me come along, didn't they? That counts!) The next day was a little more eventful, at least for my grey companion.

I didn't really know what our Amsterdam plans were before I arrived. But I soon found out. We were to check out of our hotel at noon, go to a screening of Roman's latest movie for all the top Dutch distributors, go to a taping of some Dutch quiz show that Roman had agreed to appear on to promote the movie, have dinner with the TV people and some of the distributors, and then catch a late plane to Paris.

It all sounded great except for one thing. What in the world was I going to do with Norton from noon till ten o'clock at night?

Since I didn't really have a choice, I simply took him with me.

The first highlight of the day was our introduction to the distributors. We were in a large screening room and were seated at a podium toward the front of the room. The studio publicity person assigned to Roman gave a little speech, telling everyone how excited they all should be to be distributing another Polanski film. He went through the litany of Roman's successes in Holland – from his *Knife in the Water* days through *Chinatown* and *Tess*. 'And now,' he said to the crowd, 'I would like to introduce some very special guests. To my right is a man who needs no introduction. One of the great directors of our time, Roman Polanski.'

There was a great burst of applause.

'To Mr Polanski's right is the writer of Mr Polanski's new film, which they are going to Paris to begin work on – Peter Gethers.'

I got some polite applause, considering no one had ever heard of me and probably would never hear of me again. And then came the best announcement, as the publicity person realized there was one other introduction he had to make.

'And to Mr Gethers's right is . . . his *cat*???'

Rarely have I heard anyone sound as confused. And rarely have I been as proud of my cat. Norton didn't exactly take a bow at the mention of his name, but he did sit up as straight as he possibly could when he heard the very puzzled-sounding applause.

We spent the rest of the day at the taping of the quiz show.

The name of the show translated into 'Wanna Bet?' It was the most popular TV programme in Holland (also in Germany and Belgium). The only way I can possibly describe it is as a cross between 'Truth or Consequences', 'Laugh-In' and the ever-popular Vegas review, *Nudes on Ice*.

'Wanna Bet?' is ninety minutes long and takes about three hours to shoot. Of those three hours, Norton spent two-and-a-half sitting next to me in the audience – the producers were nice enough to give him his own seat – mostly staring at the flashing sign, which, I assume, said 'Applause' in Dutch.

The other half-hour he spent in the dressing room – where I was not allowed – being petted by the thirty gorgeous and statuesque topless dancers who participate in the show's sketches.

Norton doesn't usually allow strangers to pick him up and carry him off, but when one of the nearly naked women rushed over to him during a break and asked permission to bring him backstage, he didn't even wait for my OK. He hopped onto the ground and followed her, without so much as a backward glance at his envious dad. When he was returned to him at the end of the show – by three dancers, none of whom could bear to part with him – it was yet another time in our relationship when I was very sorry Norton didn't speak English. From the look on his face, however, even if he did, I wasn't ever going to get the details of this particular adventure.

When the show was over, we went to dinner with the heads of the TV studio and several of the distributors who'd earlier been introduced to Norton.

We were taken to one of the city's top restaurants. Norton came along as if he were accustomed to dining out every evening. He hadn't been near his litter box in hours and hours *and* he'd never been out to eat in public, so I was a tad nervous. However, my boy came through with flying colours. He was the hit of the evening.

The first thing that happened was that our

173

waitress practically fainted when she saw how cute Norton was. When she saw how calmly he sat on my lap, she insisted on bringing him his own chair, which she slipped in next to mine. Next, she brought him his own dinner – a nice little plate of herring and potatoes, which Norton gobbled down appreciatively. He was having such a good time that I was almost insulted when she didn't offer him a glass of wine – although he did seem a lot happier with his dish of milk.

This was supposed to be a business dinner, with Roman talking up his movie, but very little business was discussed. Most of the conversation centred around the newest – and smallest – guest of honour. Every few minutes, someone would insist on switching seats with me or Roman, who was on the other side of Norton, so he or she could be near the cat. By the end of the evening, I was on the complete other end of the table, Norton was in between the head of the Dutch film distribution industry and the woman producer of 'Wanna Bet?', doing his best Cary Grant impersonation – politely chewing on his herring, sipping his milk, sitting up in his chair, and basically appreciating the restaurant and the attention.

When it was time to leave, several people offered to let Norton stay in their homes if I ever came through the city again, and several asked if they could visit him on their next trip to New York. By the time we boarded the plane for Paris, he was one exhausted cat. In fact, I had to wake him up as we circled over the city, holding him up to the window so he could get his first glimpse of the brightly lit Eiffel Tower.

Norton took to Paris like, well, like a *canard à l'eau*.

We stayed at one of my very favourite hotels in the world, the Tremoille, which is on the corner of Rue de la Tremoille and Rue du Boccador in the eighth arrondissement. It is gorgeous, it is small, it is elegant, friendly, it is *very* Parisian *and* they *love* my cat.

Last year, when I was writing another movie with Polanski, my agent, Esther – she of Norton's very first plane ride – popped into Paris for a couple of evenings of fun and good food. I was there for three months and, to my regret, wasn't staying at the Tremoille – the studio had decided it was too expensive for such a long stay, so I got an apartment – but I insisted that *she* stay there. After dinner, I walked her back to the hotel and talked about how nice they always were to Norton. As I was elaborating, she stopped me on the street and said, 'I don't believe you. You are definitely making this up.' Indignant, I insisted I was absolutely telling the 100 per cent truth. She refused to accept this. So when we reached the lobby, I went up to the front desk, smirked confidently at Esther, and said to the concierge, 'Good evening. Do you remember me?'

'Of course,' he responded. 'And 'ow is your leetle cat? Is 'e well?'

'Very well,' I told him.

'Please send him my best,' the man said, to

Esther's total astonishment. 'Tell 'im to come visit anytime 'e weeshes.'

Esther now believes everything I tell her.

Over the years, Norton has stayed at the Tremoille six or seven times, usually when I'm working with Roman. Our writing routine is as follows: start around ten-thirty or eleven in the morning, break for lunch at one o'clock or so, a nice leisurely lunch, then work from three until seven or eight. After an hour or two-hour break to relax, to have a glass of icy Polish vodka, or just to get away from each other, we usually have dinner. I'd always go back to the hotel to check on and play with Norton, either during our lunch break or our pre-dinner break. After a while, I realized that playtime was unnecessary. Norton didn't need any more playing with. Almost every time I returned to the room, there was at least one maid, usually two, petting him, scratching him, playing with some new toy they'd just bought for him. Once he became an accepted member of the hotel family, they let him hang out in the lobby during the day (one of the people on the desk or one of the maids would bring him back to the room if they felt things were too hectic) and let me bring him down to the formal dining room for dinner.

One day there was a near catastrophe. I came back at 7 p.m. for my daily check-in, strolled jauntily into the hotel, and asked for my room key. One of the managers looked at me very gravely and said, 'Oh, Monsieur Gethers, your leetle cat, he is very seek.'

Without another word, I grabbed the key and raced up the two flights of stairs to my room. When I ran inside, a maid was sitting on the bed, soothingly petting Norton and cooing at him. He was snuggled up on my pillow, curled into a ball. All in all, he looked pathetic – and was clearly sick.

The maid didn't speak any English, so I didn't catch all of what she said. Basically, I picked up on the fact that she'd come into my room early that morning to clean, began her usual play routine with Norton, only he didn't respond. He wouldn't leave the bed, he wouldn't pick his head up, he wouldn't move at all. She tried to give him some Pounce – I'd brought over a lifetime supply and had shown all the maids where I kept it – and he wouldn't even touch that. This was serious.

Norton had never, ever been sick before. I didn't know what to do. Roman was surprisingly understanding when I told him I was going to skip our usual dinner and carousing because of a sick cat. He was pretty attached to Norton by this time, too.

Norton didn't eat that night. Nor did he move from my pillow (I slept on his side of the bed all night). I did my best to reassure him that everything was going to be all right, but he was not a happy kitten. If you ever hear anyone say that cats don't think or feel, all you have to do is tell them to spend the night in bed with a sick one. If you looked up the word 'mournful' in the dictionary, you would have seen a picture of Norton that night. I decided to give him twenty-four hours before calling a French vet.

He seemed to be feeling better the next morning. (I, on the other hand, wasn't doing too well since I'd tossed and turned with worry all night.) He wasn't particularly active – he wouldn't get out of bed to eat his breakfast – but he did munch on a couple of Pounce when I brought them to him, and he did lick my hand appreciatively afterwards. When I left to go to work, Norton roused himself slightly, standing up for a moment on the bed. I came back, told him he'd be fine, and then watched him settle back onto my pillow.

At lunchtime, I came back to see how Norton was feeling. The manager gave me the thumbs-up sign when I picked up my key. Sure enough, in the room were two maids, hovering over Norton, who was now resting playfully on his back, enjoying their gentle scratching and friendly babbling. They had bought him a present – a little catnip tree, which they'd placed on the end table by the bed. They told me that he wasn't quite ready for it, but they thought it would be a good incentive for him to get well.

I went back to work knowing my pal was in good hands. At that night's dinner break, he was back to normal. Not only did he gulp down his dinner and leap at the Pounce when I held it out to him, he munched a few leaves off his new catnip tree. When it was time for bed, he was well enough to sleep on his own pillow. I had no idea what had brought on his one-day illness – perhaps it was all that rich French cat food – but with a sigh of relief, I told him I was glad he was feeling better and kissed him on the top of his head. He gave me a quick lick with his sandpaper tongue and made me feel as if, at the very least, I'd been an understanding and supportive nurse.

We fell into a fun Parisian routine, Norton and I. Since I didn't have to be at work until at least ten-thirty, I got into the habit of going to one particular café, across the Seine from the Eiffel Tower, for my morning *café au lait*. After a few mornings of this, I didn't see any reason not to take Norton. So every day he'd hop into his shoulder bag, we'd leisurely stroll the few blocks to my regular haunt, and I'd sit in my straw café chair, sipping coffee and reading the *Herald Tribune* while he sat in his chair, sphinxlike, watching the passersby and, once the waiters got used to his presence, lapping at a small bowl of water or milk.

After breakfast, I'd usually take him back to the hotel. Sometimes I'd take him over to Roman's apartment. That first trip, when I was rewriting the script for what became the film *Frantic*, Harrison Ford came over to spend a couple of weeks working with us. He was the star of the film and, as such, quite properly wanted to have input into character motivation, action and thought. He and Roman were friends but had never worked together. I'd never met Harrison before. So the first few days were spent feeling each other out, seeing how we'd all get along, all of us trying to be firm with our convictions for the movie, yet flexible and sensitive to the other two's egos and desires. Harrison has a reputation – which my experience certainly bears out – for being a remarkably intelligent actor. It's remarkable because actors, in general, are not considered much higher on the intelligence scale than your basic, everyday dining-room table. They are also known for screwing up scripts in order to make their characters look better. Not only is Harrison smart, he's more concerned with the *movie* than whether or not his character is braver, brighter and cleverer than all the other characters. I liked him and respected him a lot right from the beginning. However, my guess is that Harrison wasn't overly impressed with me the first day he showed up. We shook hands, started discussing the first draft of the script, which was written by Roman with his longtime collaborator, Gerard Brach – what was wrong with it and what was right with it – and then, just as we were really getting into it, just as some passion was coming out in the conversation, Roman started sniffing the air.

'What smells so terrible?' he asked.

'Wait. Hold it,' Harrison said, getting excited. 'I think I'm onto something here. I think this guy, this doctor, has to really love his wife, has to be *incredibly* jealous of her—'

'Whoooo, what could smell so bad?' Roman was clearly distracted. His face was scrunched up as if breathing were a painful matter.

'Roman, Roman, listen to me! I think we need a scene between me and my wife, something tender, right at the beginning . . . Jesus, what *is* that smell?'

Eventually, all discussion of the script stopped. The entire apartment was starting to smell as if someone had died – about three weeks ago. Both heads turned to me when I muttered quietly under my breath, 'Uh . . . I think I know what it is.'

I marched them into Roman's bathroom. There in the tub sat my cat. There next to him sat a very large pile of . . . well . . . what can only be described as cat shit.

'I forgot to bring his litter box today,' I explained meekly. 'He usually goes in the tub when there's no litter box.'

'That's pretty smart,' Roman noted.

'This is *your* cat?' Harrison asked.

I nodded.

'You brought him from New York??'

I nodded again.

'I'm working with a writer who brings his cat to Paris so he can shit in the bathtub?'

'I know it looks bad,' I said, 'but give him a second chance.'

'It's not *him* I'm worried about,' Harrison said to me.

This was my introduction to a lifetime's fantasy – writing a movie in Paris with a brilliant director and a superstar actor: the brilliant director and the superstar actor on their knees in the bathroom trying to scrub away the smell of cat shit while I held the cat, trying to assure him that he hadn't done anything wrong.

Over the years, I believe Norton has come to prefer Paris to New York, much like his dad. He likes his morning alfresco breakfasts; he enjoys his occasional restaurant dinners. (By coincidence, Norton and I were in Paris when I signed the contract to do this book. He *definitely* enjoyed the celebratory dinner I took him to that night. We went to my very favourite joint, L'Ami Louis, where Norton received his own giant plate of Louis's specialty, the best foie gras one could ever hope to eat.) This cat has even been to a nightclub or two. I will go out on a limb and say, absolutely, that he is the only cat ever to have danced the night away at Bains Douches, one of Paris' very coolest clubs. A lot of people get turned away by the doorman at Bains Douches – but Norton has guaranteed entry when he shows up.

One of my little cat's favourite pastimes was exploring the famous rooftops of Paris. He had access from our room at the Tremoille. The hotel has those old-fashioned, very heavy windows that swing open. (Wait a second – perhaps, at last, I understand why they're called *French* windows!) Norton used to sit with his nose pressed up against the bedroom window, just waiting for me to get the hint that he was desperate to go outside. At first I was hesitant, but once again logic lost out to a cat's desire and the window was thrown open. I held Norton in my arms for a few moments, explaining to him that he was in a strange city and that he shouldn't go too far away – then up over the balcony he went, scrambling out onto the red tile rooftops of the city.

I don't know how far he actually travelled. I

once saw him three peaks away – perhaps half a block. He always came back when called, so he couldn't have been out of hearing distance. Eventually, I relaxed with his outdoor prowling, and as soon as I could get the maids to understand that if he wasn't in the room, they shouldn't ever shut the windows, I even began leaving them open during the day so he could strut his stuff when I wasn't there.

The other thing Norton enjoyed for a while was our unusual Paris/New York commute. Although it's usually a safe rule of thumb for a writer to assume that everything he does is either going to fail or never come to fruition, there was a stretch of about a month where everything I was working on happened at the same time – the Polanski movie, a novel I'd written, a TV pilot – and Norton and I spent this particular February practically living on the Concorde. Once a week I'd go to Paris for a few days to work on the screenplay. Then I'd hop back on the speedy plane, zip back to New York, do whatever I was doing there – I could barely tell one activity from the other by this point – and then head to the airport and jump back on the Concorde. I would spend the quick flight either reading, writing, or rewriting. Norton would spend the few hours wandering around the small cabin, making friends with the attendants and fellow passengers.

This was definitely the height of luxury for a cat and the highlight of his European travels. The Concorde attendants got to know him so well they didn't even make me bring his box.

After a while, all I needed was his cloth shoulder bag. He was so much at home on the plane that I half-expected, on one of the flights, to hear the following message over the loudspeaker: 'Ladeez and gentlemen, we have ze guest pilot for zis flight today. Monsieur, please say hello to ze passengers.' Then the pilot would come on the loudspeaker and I'd hear: 'Meow'.

Things never went that far, of course, but it wasn't for lack of trying on Norton's part.

In fact, if you're thinking of flying to Paris any time in the near future, I wouldn't rule out the possibility. If you want to make sure your plane lands on time, I suggest you bring a good supply of Pounce.

8

The Cat Who Fell in Love

My cat was getting older, and with age was coming a certain complacency, a slightly existential, lackadaisical attitude. Plus, he was starting to get fat.

So I did what any normal person would do for his cat. I bought a house.

During the summers at Fire Island, Norton would run everywhere, all the time, having a ball, and every season he would lose a pound between Memorial Day and Labor Day. By the time the leaves started to change colours, that Scottish Fold was one lean, mean fighting machine. Over the autumn and winter, however, he never left the confines of my apartment (except for the occasional cross-country ski trip), which meant he did a lot of sitting, sleeping and begging for Pounce. I knew that wasn't good for him. Since I tended to do the same thing – the lazing around part, not the begging – I suspected it probably wasn't good for me either. So I decided to go house hunting.

Well, I didn't actually house *hunt*. As usual, I house *stumbled*.

Nancy and Ziggy had a place in Sag Harbor, and I went out to visit them one weekend. Norton was supposed to be left at home because Zig is highly allergic to cats. At the last second, however, my trusty cat-sitter wimped out. (I haven't really discussed what happens when my travelling cat occasionally has to be left behind. Luckily, a friend named Lynn Waggoner has decided that sitting for Norton is comparable to chauffeuring Tom Cruise around the city. Well, perhaps I'm exaggerating, but Lynn takes awfully good care of Norton – buying him toys, taking him for walks, all those good things he's come to enjoy and expect. Once, when Lynn was unavailable, my assistant took him for a weekend. She brought him to her in-laws' house in Montauk. Norton had been in the house for all of two minutes when someone left the front door open – and Norton took off. Laura, the by-now terrified assistant, and her husband spent the night in the woods searching high and low for him. They gave up somewhere around 2 a.m. and came home – to find Norton waiting patiently by the front door. Laura later told me the story – *much* later – and also revealed her strategy on how to break it to me that she'd lost my cat. It was going to be in the form of a suicide note.) Anyway . . . since no cat-sitter was available, I surprised my weekend hosts and brought Norton after all.

My surprise was greeted with all the enthusiasm of an earthquake. He'd be no problem, I assured them. He'd stay outside the whole day. He'd come in only at bedtime, and then he'd sleep with me. I wouldn't let him out of my bed. Zig would never know there was a cat in the house.

That was true. He didn't know there was a cat in the house – until the middle of the night, when Norton, slipping away while I was asleep, went upstairs and decided he'd sleep on Ziggy's head.

That night at the Aldermans was not dissimilar from what I imagine Krakatoa must have been like. At 3 a.m. I went upstairs, grabbed Norton off the sputtering master of the house, and took him back into my bed. At 3.30 a.m. he was back on Ziggy's head. We repeated the procedure. At 4 a.m. Norton had returned to his new favourite spot, covering most of Zig's face with his entire body. At 4.30 a.m. Zig gave up. At 5 a.m. he realized he wasn't sneezing any more. By morning, he'd decided Norton was the first cat he'd ever met that he wasn't allergic to. Fury and despair turned to delight and triumph. I was not a favourite house guest (in fact, I won the poll for Most Annoying Weekender) – but somehow Norton had wormed his way into their hearts.

The next day, we went to check out the real estate. My search was only a halfhearted one. I can't say I *really* wanted a house. For one thing, I'm not the handiest guy in the world. I still wake up screaming in the middle of the night at the thought of my high school wood shop. The idea of using a drill or repairing some electrical wiring can quickly bring on my best Curly Howard impersonation, with all the face smacking, high-pitched blubbering and floor-whirling trimmings. For another, I loathed the idea of any kind of commute, even if it was just on weekends. I had no desire ever to do any gardening or to rake up leaves or to shovel snow off the driveway. In fact, I didn't even want a driveway, since I didn't own a car.

But Norton needed a year-round playpen, so . . .

The first four houses we looked at were all nice, all spacious and all wrong. They didn't have any personality or charm. The realtor, a woman named Peggy Meves, to whom I am forever indebted, asked me to describe my ideal house – my *affordable* ideal house. I did so: at least a hundred years old, in such good shape it needed no work, original wood floors and beams, a fireplace or two, eccentric rooms, two stories, an office that was so nice I'd *want* to go sit at the typewriter, a manageable size – perhaps two or three bedrooms – but not cramped and not so spacious that I couldn't take care of it. In other words, something that was so perfect I'd never find it.

When I finished my description, Peggy said, 'You know, I think you should take a look at this one place. But the people have received an offer on it. I think they've accepted, so I don't think you can have it – but it sounds like what you're looking for. At least it'll give me an idea of what your taste is like.'

I agreed to go look at the house, knowing that I couldn't buy it. That was all right with me. Again, I didn't really want to buy anything. I mostly just liked looking at nice houses.

I didn't even make it upstairs. One look at the living room – with its original 120-year-old wood floors, its antique potbellied stove, its *personality* – and I heard myself saying, 'I'll take it'.

Peggy, being that rarest of breeds, a completely honest person, tried to tell me again that I couldn't have this house. She was just showing it to me for taste purposes.

'This is my dream house,' I said. 'I think I *have* to have it.'

'At least look upstairs before you decide it's your dream house,' she advised.

Upstairs made it even worse. There was a tiny, heartbreakingly charming guest bedroom, a large master bedroom (the bathroom had an old claw tub in it!), and to round out my fantasy, there was a small office that hung over the driveway, with French windows that looked out onto the beautifully landscaped garden. I haven't even mentioned the outside of this place, which looked as if Hänsel and Gretel could have comfortably settled in and been right at home.

I ran down the steps, outside to my rented car and opened the door. Norton came bounding onto the front lawn. He stepped cautiously inside the house, looked around the living room, then plopped himself down in the middle of the floor, directly catching a ray of sunlight streaming in through the window. He looked up at me and meowed happily.

The next day, I bought the house.

All of a sudden I had a country house, I had a cat, I had good friends for neighbours. I was just missing one little thing.

Despite a rather flip exterior (hiding, many people would say, an amazingly shallow interior), I was becoming a bit concerned that Cindy's parting words – 'you don't know what love is' – had more than just the hollow ring of truth to them. I was beginning to think that too many years of going for the gag, hanging out with Danish models and working round the clock had possibly limited my capacity for 'something more'. Of course, everytime I began to think this, I tried to imagine what could be 'something more' than laughs, Danish models and satisfying work. I have quite an active imagination but, in this area, my imagination had run totally dry.

And yet . . .

There was Janis.

This was an unusual affair because Janis was not at all my type. Physically she was quite lovely but not the kind of looks I usually go for. She was short and slightly round rather than long and lean. She was extremely classy looking, elegant and sophisticated, where my taste usually ran to the slightly trashy. She was Deborah Kerr in *An Affair to Remember* as compared to my usual leaning – the soap-covered girl who washed the car in front of the prisoners in *Cool Hand Luke*. Even her personality was off-kilter alongside any past infatuations. I wasn't wild about confrontations. To say Janis was combative would be like saying Lawrence Taylor has an aggressive streak. She had the independence and confidence of British royalty and was as stubborn and opinionated as anyone this side of Saddam Hussein. Yet, despite all our differences – or perhaps because of them – she was the most intelligent, most stimulating, least boring person I'd met in a long, long time.

There was a slight hitch, however, to my having a long-lasting, perfect, satisfying relationship with Janis. She didn't *want* a long-lasting, perfect, satisfying relationship. At least, she didn't want one with me.

The closer we became, the more she'd pull back. Eventually, she pulled back so far I needed a telescope to find her. Which was a good sign the romance was over.

The relationship didn't end, however. What happened was that Janis and I became best friends. Without the threat of a romance, we became as close as two people could be. We even wound up working together. We saw each other during the day, we had dinner several times a week, we even went away on weekends together a few times – strictly platonically. She saw me through a couple of tough romances, through several professional crises. I did the same for her. Despite the Sarahs and the Karyns and the sportswriters and the Dickensian editors, it was Janis who always seemed to be there, whether the 'there' was for fun, for support, or for anything that struck either one of us as interesting. We became so inseparable that most people thought we were still a couple. But she didn't want that. She didn't want a relationship because, in her experience, relationships only pointed towards the *end* of relationships. With ending came pain (and the better the relationship, the more painful the ending). With pain came bitterness. With bitterness came sorrow. You can take it from there.

Over time, I accepted that there was never going to be any kind of real relationship with this woman. It took some doing – a lot of teeth gnashing, a good bit of stomach hurting and way too much head banging – but I did eventually accept it.

Only one person didn't accept it.

And I suppose I have to use the word 'person' loosely.

Norton liked Janis.

It was particularly noticeable because she didn't much care for him. Animals were something else she didn't want to get attached to. She didn't see the pleasure in such an attachment. She didn't see the point. But Norton didn't let up. Usually, when someone ignored him, my cat was happy to be ignored. Janis was the only person other than my father that I ever saw him pursue. When she came over, she wouldn't pet him – but within moments he'd be by her side, rubbing his body up against her leg or trying to burrow his face into the palm of her hand. Rarely did she so much as respond – but over the course of several years Norton never gave up.

Whenever he saw her, he rolled over on his back in his best impersonation of the world's cutest cat. If she refused to look at him, he'd move to her, rubbing, cuddling, purring. Janis was tough – she knew the dangers of getting involved. But Norton was tough, too – he knew the *pleasures* of getting involved.

For a lot of this period – Norton v. Janis – I was content to remain neutral. Then came Sag Harbor.

When I bought the house out there on Long Island, I had already rented a house on Fire Island with Norm for the summer. The thought of one last season avoiding the sixishes appealed to me (especially since I'd already paid for it), so I came up with the perfect solution. I arranged for Janis to live in my new house for the summer, rent-free, on the condition that she fix it up – furnish the kitchen with utensils, buy and put up drapes, start to get the garden in shape. All the things that I would never have either the time, taste, nor inclination to do. It was a fair deal and she accepted happily. At the end of the summer, Norm and I drove out to Sag Harbor to check up on the house and to have dinner with Janis. She insisted on cooking; dinner was served amidst delicate candlelight on the front porch. When I stepped inside – this was my first time there since I'd signed the papers three months earlier – I was amazed. The place was no longer just charming – it was beautiful. It no longer just had its own personality – it had Janis's. It was clear to me that she loved the house as much as I did. It was clear to anyone who bothered to look inside and see what she'd done with it.

That night we had a wonderful time. The food was delicious, we drank a lot of wine, everyone laughed until we were too tired to laugh any more, and – for the first time in several years – it didn't feel right leaving Janis. It felt as if there was unfinished business.

Driving back to the city with Norm, we discussed it. He noticed that Janis had seemed softer than usual, that her guard was down, or at least lowered (she usually had barbed wire and German Shepherds surrounding and protecting her vulnerability). We discussed the question of the homing instinct – was it actually enough to push two people into a relationship?

Norm thought that it was – if the two people were finally ready for a relationship. He also thought it was interesting that Janis had gone out of her way to do one thing she'd never done before. Right before we got in the car to head back to New York, she'd bent over the couch and petted Norton. Stroked him once, gently.

It had started to rain during our drive and I remember looking at Norton through the rear-view mirror. He was sitting comfortably in the backseat, relaxed, dozing. I wondered if I could really use a cat as a gauge for a relationship.

Norton didn't open his eyes to peer back. He wasn't going to make it easy for me.

Janis's birthday comes in the middle of September. It was on her birthday that we decided to bring our relationship to a new level. Or just bring it back to what it had once been. Or bring it back but make it different. As you may gather, we weren't exactly sure *what* we were doing.

What I *am* sure of is that whatever we were doing or becoming, we wouldn't have done it or become it without Norton.

My house became *our* house – mine, Janis's and Norton's. Norton was fun to be with on the weekends in Sag Harbor and he made us both laugh. Janis couldn't get over the fact that he'd walk with me to Sean's Murray Hill Market, three blocks away from the house. Unlike Fire Island, Sag Harbor had traffic, so it was difficult to get him to take mid-afternoon strolls. But early in the morning, before cars started clogging up the streets, Norton would leisurely walk along behind us, meowing forcefully as usual. He'd wait patiently outside the market while we shopped, then hike back with us. Initially, Janis would get impatient if Norton decided to duck into the bushes for a two-minute (or ten-minute, depending on his mood) time-out from the walk. She'd try to convince me to leave him behind when it was time to buy groceries. Soon, however, she was coaxing him into taking the walk with us. And once he was along for the journey, if I started walking too fast for the cat, she'd urge me to slow down. 'Don't be so impatient,' she'd lecture me. She stopped complaining when he got side-tracked and welcomed him back happily when he rejoined us.

She also liked to watch Norton prowl the

garden. There were no bluejays to torment him in Sag Harbor, but there was a mockingbird and he quickly became my kitten's new nemesis. Once the mockingbird had sized up the situation – the macho-level of the grey, furry animal in the backyard – he started zooming out of his tree, landing on the ground a few feet from Norton and then would stand there screaming at the poor cat. Norton was totally intimidated. Janis would urge him on, try to get him to beat up on the puny bird, of course to no avail. She began to take it as a personal insult and I would often find her explaining to Norton – as I had years before on Fire Island – about the law of the jungle and the concept of the food chain.

She grew catnip in the garden for him. It never got high enough for us to cut it and let it dry. As soon as she'd plant it, Norton would make a beeline for the spot, dig up the ground around it and spend a happy few hours rolling around in the dirt while Janis would mock-scold him.

It was fun to watch a relationship develop between the two of them, both so independent. I'd got used to Norton's near-magical powers over the years, so it was rejuvenating to see his effect on her and to watch her witness his effect on others.

Janis was with us one day as we were driving along the LIE out to Sag Harbor. I was driving, Janis was passengering and Norton was in his usual position, lying down in the back, staring out the rear windshield. (When just the two of us drive, Norton will sit on the front seat, but

Janis doesn't like him up there. For one thing, she thinks it's dangerous. For another – the real reason – Norton's claws will occasionally come out, to help him balance himself if the car lurches, and he will ruin her stockings or rip a small hole in her blouse. So Norton will lie patiently in the back, content to watch the countryside zip by, until Janis falls asleep. Then he'll sneak up cautiously to the front and make himself comfortable.) It was a beautiful day, I was lost in thought and, apparently, also speeding like a lunatic. When the motorcycle cop pulled us over, he already had his ticket pad in hand as he broke it to me that I was going seventy-five miles an hour. Before he could write up the ticket, though, he glanced at the backseat.

'Is that a Scottish Fold?' he asked.

I nodded. I'm much better nodding than I am talking to policemen.

'He's beautiful,' this leather-jacketed cop said. 'I have a Fold, too.'

I won't bore you with the sappy details. Suffice it to say that Norton let himself be held and petted by the arresting officer – and the arrest was never made. My record remained unblemished and the ticket was torn up.

Janis was around for another car confrontation with Norton, this one without quite the happy ending of the earlier one.

I had driven to the office that day and had decided to take the cat. He was a perfect corporate companion, spending the whole day either lying on my desk or resting on the couch in the corner.

197

Periodically, he'd wander out of my office and stroll along the hallways, stopping to visit the people he liked. It was no longer a surprise to anyone at the publishing company – even the Chairman of the Board – when a cat would wander in to say hello.

It was a brutally hot summer day, and naturally enough, the air conditioner in my car was broken. Driving home – Janis in front, Norton in the back hoping she'd doze off – all the windows were wide open. Downtown, in the Village, on the way to the garage, we stopped at a red light. On the street corner was a bag lady, filthy, kind of crazy seeming, clearly homeless. It had been a hard day at work, it was too hot, whatever the reason, when the woman came up to our car and asked for money, both Janis and I looked right through her. It was as if she weren't a real person, as if she didn't exist. Perhaps we'd been in New York too long, where homelessness is a way of life, something too easy to inure yourself against.

As the car idled, the woman asked me a question.

'Is that a special breed of cat?' she said, pointing to Norton, who was looking out at her, his paws up on the back door, his head sticking through the open window.

Without really thinking about it – except snobbily to decide I didn't want to explain Norton's pedigree to a homeless woman – I simply said, 'No. He's a regular cat.'

'Oh,' she said. 'He looks like a Scottish Fold.'

The light turned green. Before I could drive on,

she added with a wistful sigh, 'I used to have seven Siamese.'

She stuck her hand through the window, gave Norton a pat on the head, and with astonishing dignity, walked on.

Much to Norton's delight, Janis allowed him onto the front seat for the few-block drive to our garage. She even hugged him. I'm sure also to his delight, neither one of us has ever looked at a homeless person in quite the same way. It was a good cure for our haughty superiority.

Janis was also present for Norton's one and only cat fight, a sorry affair by any standards.

I had long suspected that Norton was no Rocky Marciano. In the garden, he liked to hunker down and stalk the occasional and ever-dangerous butterfly, but that was the extent of his aggressive tendencies. Unfortunately, when one rears an outdoor cat, one must face up to the fact that other outdoor cats will come a-calling.

We had noticed a large orange, furry guy who seemed to enjoy strolling around our backyard in Sag Harbor in the late afternoons. If Norton was outside for these appearances, he would either meow immediately to be let in or he'd quickly disappear around the front of the house to one of his secret hiding spots. If this bully was visiting while Norton was safely inside the house, Norton would bravely stand at the back door, protected by a screen, and hiss loudly. He'd arch his back and release his claws, then he'd look over to us for approval. Either Janis or I would tell him what a tough guy he was and how proud we were of him. Perhaps that's what made Norton cocky.

One afternoon, while sitting upstairs in my office working away, I heard the most god-awful noise. It was a wail of pain and fear and it seemed to stretch on forever. That was followed by Janis's scream. She screamed my name and then yelled for me to come downstairs.

I made it as quickly as I could, but in the few seconds it took me, I heard violent hisses and howls, high-pitched growls and what sounded like two sumo wrestlers thudding into each other. By the time I got outside, the orange monster was walking triumphantly across the lawn. I screamed at him and waved my arms. That didn't seem to scare him – he gave me a look that made it clear he felt he could take me, too – but he did get the message that he wasn't welcome. Once he had hurdled the fence and landed in my neighbour's yard, I went looking for Norton.

Now, my cat *always* comes when I call him. *Always*. But not this time. Janis and I spent twenty minutes searching for him high and low. No Norton. I really began to be afraid when I finally heard a very soft and rather pathetic meow. I stopped and listened, heard it again. So did Janis. It seemed to be coming from under my car, which was parked in the driveway.

I got down on my hands and knees to look, and sure enough, Norton was cowering there. It took several more minutes of coaxing, but I finally got him to come. When he slunk out between the rear tyres, Janis gasped. Norton was bleeding above the nose and on his right shoulder. His fur was matted and sticky and he was so frightened, he seemed to have curled up to half his normal size, which wasn't very big to begin with. When I picked him up in my arms, I realized he had been so terrified, he had also defecated, somehow all over himself.

I calmed him down as best I could, then carried him upstairs to the bathroom. Putting him down in the bathtub, I turned on the water, just a gentle stream from the tap and did my best to clean him up. He made no effort to resist. Once he was clean, I could see that his scratches and scrapes were minor. The physical wounds were surface, but the emotional scars seemed to run deep. After I dried him off, talking to him and cooing at him the whole time, he timidly went into my bedroom, hopped onto the bed and crawled under the covers. He burrowed his way to the foot of the bed and stayed there for the rest of the afternoon. Every so often, I'd try to get him to come out, but, ashamed, he wouldn't even look at me. By dinnertime, he still hadn't poked his head out from under the quilt.

At that point, Janis decided the situation called for a woman's touch. I watched as she sat on the bed and gently pulled the covers back. Norton curled up into a ball, his face hidden. But where he had refused to look at me when I'd tried to cheer him up, he slowly began to uncurl as Janis stroked him and whispered to him. Within a few minutes, his little tongue was out, licking her fingers. When she told him it was now time to come downstairs and eat dinner, he rose, jumped off the bed and followed her down the steps.

It took Norton a couple of days before he was up to snuff. He didn't look me in the eye for quite a while. Somehow it was more humiliating for him to face his dad than his new mom after his run-in with the orange Chuck Norris. I did notice a new bond between Norton and Janis after that. Somehow, he trusted her more than he had before. And somehow, she knew it and responded in kind.

Because Janis was so resistant to a relationship, it was easy to chart her ups and downs by her responses to the cat. When she would be overcome by fear or the claustrophobia of a relationship, she would push Norton away. When she was feeling affectionate towards me, it was easier to show it to the cat. It was safer.

Our biggest arguments at the beginning were over Norton's sleeping arrangements. She *hated* that he slept with us. I had reached the point where I couldn't sleep well if he wasn't in the bed with me. She felt smothered by him – especially because he insisted on sleeping directly to her left, by her head. Since I was directly to her right, she was caught smack dab in the middle of us – for eight hours a night.

Norton would get in bed before either of us, usually settling down on Janis's pillow (he still slept like a person – head on the pillow, body under the covers). She'd crawl into bed before I would, pick Norton up and unceremoniously toss him onto the floor. I'd finally come in, ready for lights–out, call for my pal and he'd come running. He'd start out sleeping by my side, but as soon as it was feasible – which meant as soon as Janis was asleep and couldn't protest – he'd move to her side. She'd start out distant and comfortable, only to wake up in the middle of the night surrounded again.

The First Stage of softening came when she stopped dumping Norton off the bed. She started moving him over to my pillow instead. Then she'd go crazy watching me try to get into bed without disturbing him.

'He's just a cat!' Janis would say. 'Throw him off!'

'No, he's too comfortable,' I'd say while I was trying to squeeze my tired body into two feet of available space.

'Get rid of him!' she'd say scornfully – but we were both aware that *she* hadn't got rid of him.

This stage lasted a long time. Over a year. It was the period in the relationship when neither person knows whether what they have together is permanent, but each is starting to think it *might* be, if such a thing as permanency is humanly possible. She wasn't throwing anything away – not me nor my cat – but she wasn't exactly embracing anything either.

During this period, our relationship grew and strengthened – we both relaxed; we both stopped trying so hard and just accepted what was – and so did Janis's relationship with Norton.

Stage Two arrived when I came upstairs one night to find Janis asleep, Norton curled up against her – on *her* side of the bed. He was taking up half her pillow. She hadn't moved to accommodate him, but she hadn't moved him away from her. It was about that time that she first told me she loved me.

Stage Three came months after that, soon after the infamous cat fight. Exhausted, I had fallen asleep early, long before Janis was ready for bed. Norton, overjoyed that he had me all to himself, plopped himself down directly in the middle of her pillow and got into our old sleeping position, me with half the bed, him with half the bed.

I didn't really fall into a deep sleep, so I was half-awake when Janis finally crawled under the covers. I was conscious enough to watch her carefully climb over the sleeping Norton – *very* carefully, so as not to disturb him. Exactly as I had done so many times over the years, she scrunched herself into two feet of sleeping space, wedging herself between me and the cat. I fell asleep soon after I felt her gently kiss my forehead – and saw her put her ear against Norton to listen to his purring, then softly kiss him good night.

It was around this time that we began to realize we might be spending a good chunk of our lives together.

Stage Four came about in a complicated and roundabout way. One thing I can say about it is that it was certainly a good test of the relationship. It all happened because I agreed to take my cat *back* to Paris.

It started with another phone call from Roman Polanski, who called to say he thought we should write something together. Not a rewrite – this time he wanted to do it from scratch.

We decided we would adapt a book. Neither one of us was brimming over with wonderful, original story lines and we thought an adaptation would be fun, easy and, from a technical standpoint, interesting. Within moments of this decision, I thought of a book I wanted to adapt. It was brilliant, it was dramatic, it was wonderfully funny and tragically sad. I pulled it down from my bookshelf, stared at it for several seconds and then stuck it right back where it came from. Too weird, I decided. They'll think I'm crazy. The book was *The Master and Margarita* by Mikhail Bulgakov. I never mentioned it to anyone. Not to Roman, not to the studio.

I didn't find another book. Neither did Polanski. The studio kept sending us thrillers. The director kept rejecting them. Then, a full year after we'd decided to work together, Roman called me. 'I know what I want to do,' he said. 'Have you ever heard of a book called *The Master and Margarita?*'

I thought it had to be a joke. He assured me it wasn't. My heart soared and two weeks later Norton and I were in Paris adapting one of the greatest literary works of the twentieth century. I do not know if our screenplay will ever get made. Probably not is my guess. Too expensive and too weird. No chance for a sequel. Those are the vagaries and frustrations of working in the movie biz. But I do know one thing about that job:

It was not easy.

The work was torturous. (Or at least as torturous as writing can be. I don't like ever to confuse writing clever dialogue with fighting oil fires or harvesting the rice paddies.) Roman is obsessive about research and meticulously faithful to whatever material he's working from. He read the novel in English. Then he read it in American (they are two different translations). Then in Polish, French and finally, Russian. Every time he read a different version, it would spark a different idea or direction. With every new idea, there was a new night I spent working – and working alone; night-time for Roman was definitely not for working – until 2 or 3 a.m.

Thank God for Norton. Never had I appreciated having him around quite so much. Most evenings, I'd come back from a day at Polanski's spent and exhausted, intellectually and emotionally drained. I'd collapse on the bed for an hour or two, Norton cuddled up against my side; then I'd order room service or take Norton out to a café for a quick bite – then back to the apartment for several hours huddled over the typewriter, trying to make sense of the day's notes and decisions. Norton would sit on the desk, directly to my left, watching me struggle, trying to whip this book into shape. By ten in the morning I was supposed to have new scenes, new ideas, new dialogue for Roman to see.

As I worked, trying to make sense of this twisting, turning novel, as I talked it over with Roman – and over and over – something started to click. The morass of political and intellectual theories that abound in the book started to come into a very definite focus. As we wrote and discussed and argued and yelled and struggled, this great and dense fantasy of a novel began to make sense to me in a way it never had before. Oddly enough – *very* oddly, since my life could not be farther from the lives depicted in the book – the sense of the book and the meaning of the screenplay came from the relationship that had developed with Janis. And, yes, with Norton.

The Master and Margarita was written during the 1930s, finished in 1939, and it was considered finished only because the author died, blind and destitute, a victim of Stalin's repression. It is easy to tell what happens in this novel. It is not easy to tell what it's about. The main characters are the Devil, a suicidal writer, a bad poet, a six-foot cat in a top hat and waistcoat, Jesus Christ, Pontius Pilate and the most beautiful woman in the world. There are brutal murders, public humiliations, crucifixions and a confrontation with the ultimate evil. There is also sharp satire, laugh–out–loud slapstick, political parody, religious revisionism, and devastating philosophical insight. There are ghosts and people flying through the air and magical transformations. Oh – it also happens to be one of the greatest love stories ever written. All in all, I suppose it's understandable that so far it's been difficult to get a Hollywood studio to give this movie a financial green light: we're not exactly talking sequel to *Home Alone*.

Anyway, after much sifting, sorting, researching, cutting and stalling, I ultimately made a decision about what *The Master and Margarita* is all about. It all came back to Cindy and her parting words of years before.

You don't know what love is.

Thanks to that trip to Paris, thanks to Janis and our developing relationship, mostly thanks to a little grey cat with a round head and folded ears, I *do* know what love is. I not only know what it is, I've found it. I've seen it work and seen what it can do.

Days before I wrote the ending to the script, I got a call from Janis. She was out in Sag Harbor. It was early in the morning her time, early afternoon for me.

'What are you doing up so early?' I asked.

'I couldn't sleep,' she told me. 'I haven't been sleeping well lately.'

'Why not?' I wanted to know.

'I miss you,' she said.

As perhaps you've noticed, I'm a sucker for this kind of stuff. 'Awww,' I said. 'That's so nice.'

'But it's not *just* that,' she added.

'What else?'

'I don't sleep well any more unless Norton sleeps by my side.'

So it was Janis reaching Stage Four that gave me the nerve to decide that our screenplay for *The Master and Margarita* should be, above all, about love. Love in its most real sense. Love between two people. Two real people. Love surviving politics and oppression and art and history and cruelty and even death. The script for the movie ends the way Bulgakov ends his book. The Master and Margarita ascend, not to heaven but to a world of two, where they can escape the often vicious and always absurd world to which we are born.

My interpretation of this great novel was that the most important thing any of us can do is to live in a world where love is a greater priority than pain. Only in my case, as now in Janis's, it is not just a world of two. As I am reminded by Norton, who this very moment sits on my desk, six inches to my left, watching me write these words, it is very definitely a world of three.

9

The Cat Who Went to Los Angeles

All of our lives, those of us who live in Western civilization, are not really so very different. We all suffer the same constraints – of time, of strength, of laws, of expectations. Within each life there are purely individual peaks and valleys, wild swings of ecstasy and despair, great triumphs, noble failures, yet, taken as a whole, there is a definite commonality of experience. The thrills we experience, which we feel no one can ever appreciate the same way, are thrills experienced by everyone – love, sex, success. The sadness that envelops us, in such a life-changing way that we are sure we are unique in the power of our feeling, envelops us all – illness, separation, poverty, death.

There are two ways to go after experiencing one of these highs or lows – one can either withdraw into isolation, or one can accept the commonality and use it as a way of learning more about ourselves and others.

Last year I experienced my first of these sadnesses. Last year my father died.

My mother called, a few days before Thanksgiving. His lung cancer, which had once spread to the hip but which had been dormant for several years, had returned and had spread even further. It had recently crushed his hip like an eggshell and was now riddling his back. My father had returned to the hospital, the pain was unbearable, and the feeling was he didn't have long to live.

Norton and I were on a plane the next day. The stewardesses, perhaps sensing my sadness, never said anything when I let the cat out of his box and onto my lap. He spent the whole flight sitting there, letting me pet him, occasionally licking my fingers with his rough little tongue.

I remembered when my dad had had his first operation. He'd had a lung removed. We were all terrified of what would happen, and Norton and I had flown out then, too. When my dad got out of the hospital, he was in tremendous pain. Every breath was agony and the only way he could get comfortable was to sit back in a giant, ugly, cushiony Barcalounger that my mother bought just for this purpose. He would sit back, practising breathing with one lung, trying to cope with the agony of broken ribs (that's how the surgeons get to the lung, through the ribs). What I remember most was how afraid my father was. Afraid of death, sure, but even more afraid of the pain.

The Barcalounger was set up in my parents' bedroom, at the foot of their bed. My dad would lie there for most of the day, watching television, the pain spoiling the concentration required even to read.

He'd been set up in the chair like this for two, maybe three days, spending most of those days just being afraid. I was in my room, maybe forty feet away, when I heard my dad call my name. It wasn't a friendly call, or even a weak one, at least not as weak as he'd been sounding. It was a fearful call and I came running.

When I got to his room, I saw what my father was afraid of. Norton was crouched below his chair, ready to leap, eyeing the blanket on my father's lap. It looked like an inviting spot to sit and be petted – especially since these two had long ago befriended each other. But my father's face was not a friendly one. He was afraid that Norton would jump on him, would jostle him, would possibly even land right on the long, jagged scar, and hurt him even more. My father was too afraid even to move.

I didn't get to Norton in time to stop him. When I came into the room, he somehow took my presence as further encouragement. And so he jumped.

I distinctly recall feeling frozen in time, as if everything were moving in slow motion. The cat was floating through the air, aimed at my father's chest. My father was staring aghast, perhaps as afraid as he'd ever been in his whole life.

Of course it was over in a split second. Norton landed on the cushioned arm of the chair, not even touching my father. My dad sagged back, exhausted from the effort of being so afraid, and Norton, ever so gently, as if he weighed not a pound, settled onto my father's lap and began to lick his hand. My dad, trembling, used his other hand to pet my cat. The blood came back into his face and finally he looked at me. He smiled – not much of a smile but a smile – and nodded weakly.

I came back an hour later to check up on him. My father was asleep now, his head back in the chair, his body relaxed. His hand was still resting on Norton's body, and Norton was still curled on the blanket in his lap. My dad woke up when I came into the room, and he smiled again. This time a real smile. Somehow he didn't look as afraid. I think he felt a little foolish that he'd been so terrified of Norton. At the same time I think he was relieved. The possibility of pain had been very real, yet the pain hadn't materialized. I actually think that moment was the first time my father thought he might get better, the first time he realized he wasn't going to die.

Three years later, as I saw him in the hospital room, he *was* going to die and this time he knew it.

My brother Eric and my mother had been under an incredible strain, living with this pressure day to day, so I was, by reason of being the newest and freshest face on the scene, elected designated strong person. The decisions weren't pleasant ones – levels of medication, when to stop the therapy, when to stop fighting and give in to the inevitable. Within a few days there weren't many more decisions to make, however. There was very little to be done. My father was in and out of lucidity, usually out. In a ghoulish way, we actually got some laughs out of the situation – final proof that I was right and Sarah was wrong: there don't seem to be any inappropriate times to find humour.

At one point, my dad, totally under the influence of pain-killing drugs, mostly morphine, was convinced Pete Maravich was playing basketball in the hall. (My dad had never met Pete Maravich to any of our knowledge; however, as Eric pointed out, since Maravich had died several months before this, it probably wasn't a good omen.) In one coherent moment, my dad was confused by the hallucinations he'd been seeing on the wall – confused because they'd suddenly disappeared. 'But they were so beautiful,' he said.

'At last,' I told him, 'you can understand why Eric and I took all those drugs back in the sixties and seventies.'

'So *this* is why,' he said. And then he said, 'Now what I don't understand is why you *stopped*.'

My dad did not want to die in the hospital. So when we knew there was nothing else the doctors could do, we brought him home.

A round-the-clock nurse had set up a hospital bed in his bedroom and that's where he settled.

The bed was near his old Barcalounger. For the several days he stayed alive at home, Norton never left that Barcalounger. He stayed there all day; he slept there at night, keeping my dad company.

One night I wanted him in my bed. It was late, maybe 2 a.m., and I wanted the company. I slipped into my dad's room. He was asleep – rather, by this time he'd slipped into a semi-coma – and the nurse was reading. Norton sat in the chair, awake, staring at my father as if waiting for word that he was allowed to jump onto his bed and comfort him. The word didn't come, at least not while I stood watching. I didn't bring Norton back into my room. I left him there in the chair and went back to sleep on my own. Just in case the word did come, I figured he might as well be prepared.

The next day my father died. It was in the late afternoon.

I wasn't there. I'd gone out shopping for groceries. Somehow, pulling into the driveway, I knew. When I stopped the car, my brother and my mother came out of the house. They were crying. I'd missed it by just a few minutes. Eric had been by his side. One minute he was breathing deeply, asleep, the next minute the breaths stopped. That's all there was to it.

I'd said my goodbyes a couple of days before. My dad had been slipping in and out of consciousness. When conscious, sometimes he would call for one of us, or all of us. Sometimes when the nurse told us he was awake, we'd just come in, never knowing if it was our last opportunity to speak or listen.

At some point, the nurse told me that he was awake and I should say whatever it was I wanted to say to him. She said I might not have another chance. So she left the room and I stood next to my dying father, holding his cold, clammy hand. I knew he knew who I was. He couldn't talk by this point, but he was smiling, rolling his eyes as if to say, 'What a bitch, huh?'

I didn't have anything to say to him. We'd been very close when he was alive – I mean *really* alive, not barely alive – and I'd said a lot to him when it meant something. I didn't have to tell him I loved him. He knew that. I didn't have to tell him I'd miss him. He knew that too. Anything I could say to him now would somehow seem fake or overly dramatic or ultimately meaningless. So I didn't say anything. I just held his hand and waited until he fell back asleep. My dad was never one to tolerate the bullshit. I think he preferred the silence.

That afternoon, Janis had arrived from New York. My dad had been crazy about her and vice versa. They had a great relationship, a lot of banter back and forth. He gave her a very hard time and she returned it with gusto. He appreciated anyone who could give him a hard time.

When she came up the stairs, the whole family was sitting around my dad's bed. He'd been unconscious, but when she walked in he seemed to stir. He was always a bit of a ladies' man.

'Dad,' I said, 'it's Janis. Janis came here to see you.'

He lifted his head, saw us all, then saw her. She smiled at him. He looked back at my mother, at my brother, at me – and rolled his eyes. A big, exaggerated roll, done for Janis's benefit. The roll said, 'Jesus – as if things weren't bad enough, *now* look who shows up!'

We all got hysterical; even my dad did his best to laugh. Then he fell back asleep and never woke up.

There's something comforting in the fact that his last act in life was to make people laugh. He kept his sense of humour right up to the end and it made everything a lot easier on all of us.

We didn't have a standard funeral. We had a party instead. That's the way he would have wanted it – my dad loved parties. He loved being a host.

My dad was in a wine group and the members of the group brought exquisite wine to toast him with. We had one of the best restaurants in LA cater the event. Three of Dad's closest friends gave speeches, talking about him. Their talks were wonderfully funny. I would say that, through the tears, there were as many laughs at the funeral as at any party my dad had ever thrown.

That night, after everyone was gone, after Janis was asleep, I went into my bathroom, the bathroom I'd had as a little kid and I broke down and cried. I cried for perhaps fifteen minutes, real wracking sobs. I cried until I was exhausted, until I not only didn't have any tears in me, I didn't have any emotions left at all.

When I was done, I looked up to find Norton staring at me. He'd pushed the bathroom door open with his nose and had come in to seek me out.

I picked him up, kissed him on top of the head and held him while I sat in the bathroom, staring out the window at our backyard. Norton didn't meow; he didn't even lick me. He just let me hold him as long as I wanted. I appreciated the silence, too. I wasn't in the mood for bullshit either.

I don't know how long I was in there. I do know it was almost light when I got back into bed.

I lay down, my head on the pillow, closed my eyes and went to sleep. Norton put his head on my pillow and snuggled in against my chest.

When I woke up, it was a new day. Many things had changed but not Norton. He was still asleep, still by my side, still content to let me hold him.

Afterword

Sometimes I worry that perhaps it's just *me*, that perhaps I make up all this stuff about Norton being so great, being so special. But every so often I'm reminded that that's not the case.

Not long ago, my friends Nancy and Ziggy had a baby, a truly marvellous little boy named Charlie Elroy Alderman. (Yes, if any of you are wondering, it is indeed Elroy as in 'The Jetsons'.)

Soon after Charlie was born, Nancy walked him down, in his stroller, from their house in Sag Harbor to mine. It was a Sunday morning and it was early. Ziggy was still asleep and so was Janis. This was Charlie's first trip down the block to visit his neighbours.

Nancy wheeled him up to the back door, picked him out of the buggy, and carried him inside.

Norton, who'd been napping on a kitchen chair, raised his head to check out the newcomer in his life. Nancy took her tiny little baby and held him down towards Norton.

'Look, Norton,' she said. 'This is a baby.'

Norton looked up at Charlie, took him in and sort of nodded as if assimilating the information.

There was a very long pause and then I heard Nancy gulp.

'You've finally done it,' she said to me.

'What?' I wanted to know.

'*Most* mothers would have said, "Look, Charlie, this is a *cat*".'

I started to laugh.

'Not with Norton,' I said.

Nancy started to laugh, too.

'No, not with Norton,' she agreed.

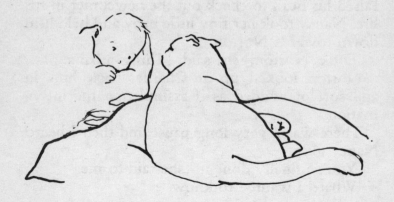

THE CAT WHO CAME IN FROM THE COLD
BY DERIC LONGDEN

'So warm and funny it'll make you want to go and get one of your own. A cat, that is'
New Woman

The little cat Deric Longden saw sitting forlornly on an upturned bucket belonged to the neighbours, but somehow when it began to rain it seemed only natural to bring him inside. Once there he slipped so easily into Deric and Aileen's lives that there was an unspoken agreement that he had found his real home. Little did he know that he had entered the Longden world, in which the unexpected (almost) always happens . . .

Aileen being Aileen, it was probably inevitable that sooner or later the kitten would be trapped in the refrigerator. And Deric being Deric, the obvious way to thaw him back to life was to make a little coat for him out of a shrunken thermal vest. Thus the cat who came in from the cold got his name – Thermal – and joined the wonderful cast of characters in the ongoing Longden saga.

Deric Longden ('the man who can make us laugh and weep in the same paragraph' – *Good Housekeeping*) has also written DIANA'S STORY and LOST FOR WORDS. Both are published by Corgi Books.

0 552 13822 3

STARLINGS LAUGHING
BY JUNE VENDALL CLARK

'In common with the very best examples of the "Africa" genre, this book is a good deal more than its spectacular sunsets, dangerous animals, diseases and droughts. June Vendall Clark's elegantly crafted autobiography . . . chronicles the struggle to establish a wildlife reserve long before it became the fashion to do so. Few books can live up to the publisher's blurb; this one does'
Observer

June Vendall Clark came to love the magic and mysticism, the wildlife, people and land of Southern Africa during the forty-three years she spent there. She lived with her philandering husband, Robert Kay, first on Far Lamorna, a farm in the Rhodesian bush, then in a converted amphibious transporter on the edge of the Kalahari Desert. For eight years June and Robert organised safaris, hunted crocodiles for a living and learned the practical lessons of survival in the wild. There were endless financial problems, tropical diseases, terrifying encounters with killer lions and the final disintegration of the marriage to contend with. But husband and wife found common cause in a battle to curb the random slaughter of wild animals. Decades in advance of today's conservation concerns, they embarked on a campaign to persuade local hunting tribes to create the Moremi Wildlife Reserve.

0 552 99426 X

replace with
attached ad
for 'Lost For Words'

JUST SOME STORIES FOR ELEANOR
BY STEPHEN PEGG

'A valiant, elegant, jovial and immensely talented writer'
Sheridan Morley

Four short years ago Stephen Pegg was a teacher enjoying an active outdoor life. Then, stiffness in one hand which he had dismissed as a sports injury was diagnosed as Motor Neurone Disease, a fatal muscle-wasting condition. He was thirty-nine.

Within a year Stephen was totally disabled – unable to move his arms or legs and virtually unable to speak. Dependent on his wife and distanced from his young daughter, Eleanor, he began to write, painstakingly tapping out the words first with a head-pointer on an electric typewriter and then on a specially adapted computer. Encouraged by his success in a national diary-writing competition, he decided to use what was left of his life to write for Eleanor, so that in years to come she would know something of her father and his love for her.

JUST SOME STORIES FOR ELEANOR, Stephen's gift to his daughter, is a collection of writings about his early life, his family and friends. Anecdotes, stories and poems form a moving and poignant testimony to the strength and optimism of a man who refused to surrender to one of the cruellest of all illnesses. Stephen died in 1991.

'A vivid and charming evocation of growing up in the fifties and sixties'
Daily Mirror

'Honest, charming, amusing and most of all, moving'
Western Daily Press

0 552 13824 X

A SELECTION OF AUTOBIOGRAPHIES
AND BIOGRAPHIES FROM CORGI BOOKS

THE PRICES SHOWN BELOW WERE CORRECT AT THE TIME OF GOING TO PRESS. HOWEVER TRANSWORLD PUBLISHERS RESERVE THE RIGHT TO SHOW NEW RETAIL PRICES ON COVERS WHICH MAY DIFFER FROM THOSE PREVIOUSLY ADVERTISED IN THE TEXT OR ELSEWHERE.

☐	99418 9	A Home by The Hooghly	Eugenie Fraser	£4.99
☐	12833 3	The House by The Dvina	Eugenie Fraser	£5.99
☐	99425 1	A House With Four Rooms	Rumer Godden	£5.99
☐	99347 6	A Time to Dance, No Time to Weep	Rumer Godden	£4.99
☐	13587 9	Every Letter Counts	Susan Hampshire	£3.99
☐	13586 0	Susan's Story	Susan Hampshire	£2.99
☐	13879 7	The Dark Romance of Dian Fossey	Harold Hayes	£5.99
☐	12863 5	The Long Journey Home	Flora Leipman	£3.95
☐	13822 3	The Cat Who Came In From the Cold	Deric Longden	£3.99
☐	13550 X	Diana's Story	Deric Longden	£3.99
☐	13769 3	Lost for Words	Deric Longden	£3.99
☐	99463 4	Dorothy: Memoirs of a Nurse	Dorothy Moriarty	£4.99
☐	13732 4	A Mother's War	Fey Von Hassell	£4.99
☐	13824 X	Just Some Stories for Eleanor	Stephen Pegg	£3.99
☐	99426 X	Starlings Laughing	June Vendall Clark	£5.99
☐	13739 1	Red Rowans and Wild Honey	Betsy White	£3.99
☐	13720 0	The Chic Murray Story	Andrew Yule	£4.99

All Corgi/Bantam Books are available at your bookshop or newsagent, or can be ordered from the following address:
Corgi/Bantam Books,
Cash Sales Department,
P.O. Box 11, Falmouth, Cornwall TR10 9EN

UK and B.F.P.O. customers please send a cheque or postal order (no currency) and allow £1.00 for postage and packing for the first book plus 50p for the second book and 30p for each additional book to a maximum charge of £3.00 (7 books plus).

Overseas customers, including Eire, please allow £2.00 for postage and packing for the first book plus £1.00 for the second book and 50p for each subsequent title ordered.

NAME (Block Letters) ....

ADDRESS ....

....